more Studies 2go

30 SOLID YOUTH BIBLE STUDIES FOR THE LEADER ON THE RUN

Julie Moser

'Let the word of Christ dwell in you richly.'

Julie Moser has been a youth minister for 18 years and is a graduate of Sydney Missionary & Bible College. She was an advisor for Anglican Youthworks in Sydney, Australia, for six years and currently works as a youth minister with her husband Ken for St John's Shaughnessy Anglican Church, Vancouver, Canada.

More Studies 2 Go Bible study sheets may be photocopied for use in local churches, youth groups and other Christian education activities. Special permission is not necessary, although the publisher respectfully requests that individual Bible study leaders each own their own copy of the book. However, no part of this publication may be reproduced, stored in a retrieval system or transmitted in any form or by any means – electronic, mechanical, photocopy, recording, or any other – except for brief quotations in printed reviews, without the prior permission of the publisher. All rights reserved.

Special thanks to Ken Moser and Steve Jeffrey.

Dedicated to: Bethany, Beth (Sass), Jess, Katrina, Natalie, Olivia (Wivs), Sam and Ali. You make Friday afternoon a highlight of the week. 1 Thessalonians 2:19-20.

© 2006 Julie Moser
This UK edition published by
The Good Book Company Ltd
Elm House, 37 Elm Road
New Malden, Surrey KT3 3HB
Tel: 0845 225 0880; Fax: 0845
email: admin@thegoodbook.co.u
website: www.thegoodbook.co.uk
Design Sarah van Delden / Anthony Wallace
Editor Laura Sieveking
Printed in China by Prosperous Printing House,
ICTI Registration No. ICTI-00946

Contents

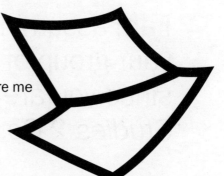

Introduction

Bible Studies

dear youth leader...

I am assuming that you have been teaching your group of young people for at least a year since you are now using the second book of *Studies 2 Go.*

I am encouraged that the first book was a useful tool for youth leaders and hope that this one will also assist you in your important ministry. These introductory notes contain material on how to make your Bible study more productive as well as give some helpful tips on writing your own studies so please read on....

Electronic copy available!

You may freely photocopy the study pages in this book. Alternatively, you can download a PDF of the study pages to print from your computer at: www.thegoodbook.co.uk/productfiles/s2g2_studypages.pdf.

The file is password protected: S2G2.

Using these studies

The introduction in the first book covered how to run a small group Bible study and how to use *Studies 2 Go* most effectively. If you didn't read these instructions the first time around let me encourage you to have a look at some stage. You may find some helpful ideas that you had not thought of that will make your small group Bible study even better.

This latest set of studies has a similar pattern to the first book. It contains studies from the Old Testament and New Testament (including a Gospel and a letter) and some topical studies. You can use these in any order you like. The 10 Commandments is a long series so you may want to split it into two halves.

The studies from John and James recommend learning a memory verse for that series. See page 78 for examples of how to learn memory verses in a fun and creative way. These are samples taken from the book: *Creative Christian Ideas* by Ken Moser. Memory verses can be great fun but are also a helpful exercise for any Christian person whether young or old.

Each study is designed for a 45 minute Bible study. However, every group is different and the study may go longer or shorter depending on factors such as the size of the group, their age and the talkativeness of the group among other things. Remember that you are not a slave to the study.

If you complete a study early you can have a longer time sharing, praying or simply enjoying each other's company. If you find you are regularly completing the study early the optional exercises before the study may be a good way to use additional time.

If you don't complete the study you can drop some sections that you have not completed and go straight to the end of the study or you can finish it off the following week. If you are regularly unable to complete the study, work out what is taking up the time. If it is because of discipline problems, lack of attention, too much talking on irrelevant topics or other problem areas you will need to address these with your group. However, the long study may be because of good reasons such as good discussion. If this is the case, work with the situation and either cut down the study in your preparation beforehand or divide the study into two halves and complete the second half the following week.

If the study is not completely suitable for your group in some way, spend some time adapting it with your own additions/subtractions to tailor it more to the needs of your group.

New feature - The Optional Exercise

A new feature of this set of studies is the optional exercises. These will be particularly helpful for those of you who run your church youth group as a Bible study or use these studies as part of your youth group program. These studies were designed for a Bible study group so you might find that the optional exercises take too much time for a midweek group. You may also find that some activities are not suitable for some reason – the good thing is that they are *optional* and not necessary to the study.

Important note

The optional exercises are mostly a fun exercise to introduce the subject and are not necessarily meant to have deep theological significance attached to it. So beware building conclusions around them – your conclusions should come from the Bible.

Another important note

The optional exercises are not meant to take up large amounts of time. Try to not to take longer than 5 – 15 minutes per exercise. Your priority is time in Bible study, sharing and prayer. If any of these activities get squeezed because of the optional activity then drop the activity. You will find that if you have an older group they may prefer to spend any extra time talking to each other – this is a much better pursuit.

Preparing and writing your own Bible study

This book of *Studies 2 Go* took much longer than I planned (or promised some of you!). So if I keep you waiting too long for the next one I have put together some step-by-step guidelines to help you write your own.

In the first book I gave you six steps to writing your own Bible study which included:

1. sharing question
2. an exercise to introduce the subject (see some examples in the studies in this book)
3. read the passage/s
4. ask some questions that will help them think through what they passage is teaching
5. apply what they have learned to their own context
6. pray

Below are step-by-step guidelines for preparation of three different types of Bible studies: Inductive, Thematic and Topical. These are very basic outlines but they give you room to make a study more interesting and creative using your own style.

Inductive

Step 1: Choose a book of the Bible or a Bible passage.

Step 2: Start with a sharing exercise (a question easily answered by all and preferably leading to the passage to be covered).

Step 3: Prepare a short introduction to the book including author, recipients, historical background and key themes. Introductions to each book of the Bible can often be found in a 'Study Bible' though a Bible Dictionary or commentary will give you more information if needed.

Step 4: Study the passage – break it into sections (paragraphs, verses, key words etc), look at specific key verses, themes and characters. Read the passage and ask some questions that will help people understand what they have read. Try not to simply ask questions that are answered by quoting the passage back to you.

Step 5: Prepare some application questions. These are questions that ask 'how does this part of the Bible challenge me in my own situation?' and 'how will your life be different because of this passage?' Without application your Bible study will only be a lecture or a comprehension exercise.

Thematic

Step 1: Choose a Bible theme, e.g. salvation, faith, grace etc.

Step 2: Write a sharing question that will help the group to share their views on the subject.

Step 3: Unless the study will do this clearly early on, give a definition of the subject to be studied.

Step 4: Choose several key passages from both the Old Testament and the New Testament – try to extract different information about the theme from these passages. Make sure you deal with the person of Jesus in your study. For example, the theme of salvation is throughout the Bible but is fully realised in the death and resurrection of Jesus.

Step 5: Prepare some application questions. Your outcome must not be simply to understand a concept but to be challenged by your new understanding from the Bible. How will your life be different because of this Bible theme?

Hint: A concordance is very handy for this kind of study.

Topical

Step 1: Choose your topic – e.g. drugs, television, love etc.

Step 2: Invite discussion that draws some conclusions regarding the opinions of the group members, their friends and families as well as society. Also work out some 'rights' and 'wrongs' on the subject.

Step 3: Using one or more Bible passages, draw conclusions about what the Bible teaches about the topic and what the view of the Christian should be. Topical studies are where the Bible is most often neglected. Make sure that your study centres around what the Bible teaches and not popular opinion. If you find it difficult to find Bible passages that speak on the topic you have chosen, ask your minister, a mature Christian you know, read some Christian books or surf the net for help.

Step 4: Prepare some application questions. Discuss how they can change wrong opinions or actions. Think of standards set by the Bible in these areas.

Some other handy hints for preparing your own studies...

1. **Before you start**, consider your group: the age, needs, Christian maturity etc and prepare appropriate material for them.

2. **Make a plan:** Do you want to do a series or a single study? Where do you want to go?

3. **Beware of using only one style of Bible study** e.g. don't just write topical Bible studies, you need to do a whole range of studies to develop a good understanding of the Christian life and faith.

4. **You can use Studies 2 Go as a model**, however, don't be afraid to branch out and develop your own style of study which suits you and your group.

5. **Invite discussion** and involvement, try not to let it become a lecture.

6. **The better you know your group, the better your Bible studies will be!** So get to know the individuals within your group.

One last thing...

If I can be a help regarding the information in this book email me at
kjmoser@hotmail.com and title the subject 'Bible Studies'.

May God continue to bless your ministry to the youth in your church
through your faithfulness to his Word.

*"Therefore, my dear brothers, stand firm. Let nothing move you. Always give yourselves fully to
the work of the Lord, because you know that your labor in the Lord is not in vain."*
1 Corinthians 15:58

Regards
Julie Moser

The 10 Commandments

Leader's Notes
You must have no other gods before me

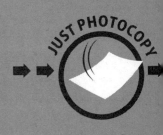
JUST PHOTOCOPY

Aim To introduce the 10 commandments and a little of their historical context. To understand that God is the only true God and we are to place him as number one in our lives. We show that he is number one by obeying him.

Personal Preparation: Read Genesis 12:1-3, Exodus and Deuteronomy 5. Also read Romans 7:7-14 and 8:1-4. If the group is not familiar with the story of Israel's slavery in Egypt and Moses you could read a brief history about how Israel had become slaves in Egypt and how God used Moses to rescue them from slavery in Acts 7:2-22 and 7:30-38.

Share: Introduce the concept of rules or laws with the two sharing questions.

Introducing the 10 Commandments

Read the short introduction and then ask for volunteers to read Exodus 20:1-17. You could also read one or two commandments each however, make sure they have the option to pass if they don't want to read.

Important note: Israel's relationship with God didn't come through following rules. God brought them into relationship with him FIRST. Israel's obedience came as a response to his love.

Optional exercise: See page 70

Commandment 1 – You must have no other gods before me

Ask everyone to tick one of the boxes that indicate how often he/she thinks about God then share their answers. Be open to discussing their answers if they want to. **Ask one person to read Exodus 20:3** and then ask each person to write this commandment in their own words and then share their answers. If this is difficult ask them how they would explain this commandment to a friend. This exercise is repeated for every study and will help the group to clarify what each commandment means. Discuss why they believe **God wants Israel to have 'no other gods' other than him.** You may like to have some responses ready. It was appropriate for Israel to recognise God as the one who rescued them from slavery. No other 'god' had done this. Ask the group to circle their responses to the five statements about following other gods and then discuss their answers. The following passage (John 14:6) will show the first two statements to be false and the third one to be true. The first commandment (Exodus 20:3) shows the last two to be false. **Read John 14:6 What does this verse teach us about following the true God?** No one comes to God except through Jesus. (Some other verses for you to be familiar with are John 3:16-18 and 1 John 5:10-12). **Ask one or more volunteers to read Mark 12:28-34** and then ask the young people for examples of loving God with their whole being. Try to help them come up with practical ways they can do this. For example when are some times they can put him first? How can they show other people that God comes first in their lives? etc.

The law and the Christian

It is important that the Christian person understands that following rules and laws does not give us a relationship with God. We fail to perfectly obey God because we are sinful however, God sent Jesus to deal with our sin. Just as God rescued Israel from slavery in Egypt, we have been rescued from the slavery of sin through Jesus' death. We now demonstrate our relationship with him through an obedient life.

Ask a volunteer to read 1 John 2:1-6 How does God deal with our failure to keep his law? (verses 1-2) He sent Jesus to take the punishment for our sin (sin=disobedience to God). **How do we show our love for God?** (verses 3-6) By living in obedience to him. **In what ways can we 'walk as Jesus did' (verse 6)?** Discus some practical examples.

Pray: Ask for help to live in obedience to God as a response to his love for us.

Challenge: Give the group one 'law' to follow this week and review next week how they went keeping that law. A good suggestion would be that they are not to think bad thoughts of another person this week.

The 10 Commandments
You must have no other gods before me

Share: What is a rule that you have to obey that you think is a stupid rule?

What is a rule that you have to obey that you think is a good rule?

Introducing the 10 Commandments

The 10 commandments are laws God gave to his people Israel for life in the promised land. God rescued his people from slavery in Egypt and they were to show their special relationship to him by obeying his laws. Read the 10 Commandments God gave Israel in Exodus 20:1-17.

Commandment 1 – You must have no other gods before me

Complete the sentence by ticking the box of one of the following statements then discuss your answers. 'I think about God...'

☐ a lot   ☐ only when I'm afraid or lonely   ☐ every now and then
☐ a few times a day   ☐ very rarely

Read Exodus 20:3 Write this commandment in your own words

• Why do you think God wants Israel to have 'no other gods' other than him?

What do you believe about following other gods?

Circle your response to each of the statements below then discuss your answers.

All religions lead to the same God	I agree	I disagree	I don't know
All religions take you to heaven	I agree	I disagree	I don't know
God has shown us one way to get to him	I agree	I disagree	I don't know
You can be a Christian and follow other gods	I agree	I disagree	I don't know
All religions agree with each other about who God is	I agree	I disagree	I don't know

Read John 14:6 What does this passage teach us about following the true God?

Read: Mark 12:28-34 Jesus summarised the 10 commandments as loving God and loving your neighbour. List some practical examples of what it means to love God with all your heart, soul and mind.

The law and the Christian

Being a Christian is not about keeping laws but about having a heart that places God as number one. Our problem is that we fail to live in total obedience to God's law. **Read 1 John 2:1-6**

• **How does God deal with our failure to keep his law?** (verses 1-2)

• **How do we show our love for God?** (verses 3-6)

• **In what ways can we 'walk as Jesus did'** (verse 6)?

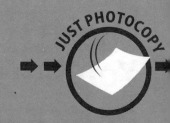

Leader's Notes
Do not make idols

Aim (By the end of the study the group will understand that God requires our total devotion to him and that we cannot love him and worship other gods. The young people will also understand an idol is more than just a statue of a god but is anything that we devote ourselves to in place of God.

Optional Quick Quiz: Try to remember all 10 commandments in order.

Review homework: Ask if anyone tried to implement the challenge to not think bad thoughts of another person for a week. Have them share their experience. The exercise should demonstrate to them our inability to live God's way and therefore we need God's mercy and help.

Optional exercise: See page 70

Share: Ask the group to write down three things they love and then have everyone share their answers. *NOTE: if you use the optional exercise you need to specify that they should not include the item they modelled with the playdoh. If you used the optional exercise you could also skip the sharing question and go straight to the study.*

Commandment 2 – Do not make idols

Ask one person to read Exodus 20:4-6 and then ask each person to write this commandment in their own words and then share their answers. Ask the young people to write their own definition for an 'idol'. An idol can be anything that can become more important than God or replaces God altogether.

What reason does God give to his people for not worshipping idols? God is a jealous God. This means that he will not compete with other gods. We are used to the word 'jealous' being used in a sinful way (i.e. when we want to have what belongs to someone else). However, when the term 'jealous' is applied to God it means that he wants an exclusive relationship with us in the same way that a husband and wife should have an exclusive relationship.

Place a number between 1 and 3 next to each of the items listed to indicate to what degree these things can become idols. (1=always tempting to worship, 2=sometimes tempting to worship, 3=never tempting to worship). Ask the group to volunteer their answers. One way of sharing answers would be to ask them to read all of their '3 list', then all of their '2 list' etc. When you are finished **discuss which of the items listed have the potential to become their idols (things that you devote yourself to instead of God).**

The idols we make for ourselves

Read the short introduction and then ask for volunteers to read Exodus 32:1-10 and 30-35. **How does God respond to the people making an idol?** He is angry and wants to destroy them and punishes their sin with a plague. This story indicates how God feels about worshipping idols.

Ask volunteers to read the two passages. After each one is read, discuss the problem with worshipping idols.

> **Isaiah 44:9-19** – An idol is nothing more than a human creation which is not able to do anything.

> **Romans 1:18-23** – Idols exchange the true God for images of things he has created. It is a denial of evidence for the true God.

How are we to respond to the idols that this world offers us today? Ask a volunteer to read Acts 17:29-31. We are to repent of this kind of ignorance. Ask if anyone would like to share something they personally would **need to change in order to keep God number one in their life.** Then discuss suggestions of how to **help each other to keep God number one in our lives** and **how we can help our friends turn from idols to the true and living God.**

Pray: that we identify those things that tempt us to ignore the true God. Pray also that we can place God above all other things in our lives.

The 10 Commandments
Do not make idols

Share: What are three things you really love (not including people).
For example: basketball, an iPod etc. Write your answers in the space below.

1. _____   2. _____   3. _____

Commandment 2 – Do not make idols
Read Exodus 20:4-6
Write this commandment in your own words:

_____

Write a definition for 'idol': _____

- **What reason does God give to his people for not worshipping idols?** (verse 5)

What idols do you think people you know are tempted to worship? Look at the list below and indicate which things people are most tempted to make into idols by rating them from 1-3 (1=always tempting to worship, 2=sometimes tempting to worship, 3=never to tempting to worship)

___ Carved statues	___ Jobs	___ Sport	___ Boyfriend or girlfriend
___ Houses	___ Physical fitness	___ Friends	___ Money
___ Cars	___ Education	___ Entertainment	___ Possessions
___ Physical beauty	___ Life of pleasure	___ Fashion	___ Internet
___ Popularity	___ Musical ability	___ Free Time	___ Other? _____

- **Which of the items listed have the potential to become your idols (things that you devote yourself to instead of God)?**

The idols we make for ourselves
God gave the commandments to Moses on Mt Sinai. While this was happening God's people waited at the foot of the Mountain. However, as they waited they grew restless. Read what they did while God was giving his laws to Moses. **Read Exodus 32:1-10 and 30-35.**

How does God respond to the people making an idol? (verses 9-10 and 33-35)

Read the following passages and work out the problem with worshipping idols:

Isaiah 44:9-19 _____

Romans 1:18-23 _____

How are we to respond to the idols that this world offers us today? Read Acts 17:29-31

- **Is there anything you need to change in order to keep God as number one in your life?**

- **How can we help each other to keep God as number one in our lives?**

- **How can we help our friends turn from idols to the true and living God?**

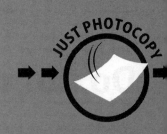
JUST PHOTOCOPY

Leader's Notes
Misusing God's name

The 10 Commandments

Aim To understand that God's name is very special and that we must not misuse it with our speech or by our actions.

Optional Quick Quiz: Try to remember all 10 commandments in order.

Optional exercise: See page 70

Share: Ask each person to share his/her full name and share any significance or meaning it might have.

Commandment 3 – Do not misuse God's name

How many names can you think of that the Bible uses for God? (e.g. the Lord, the Father). They may not be able to think of any in which case it would be helpful for you to have some prepared. Some examples are: the Lord, the Father, I am, Yahweh, God, Jehovah, the rock, the good shepherd.

Ask one person to read Exodus 20:7 and then ask each person to write this commandment in their own words and then share their answers.

Ask the young people to choose one response from the list of the responses that matches what they do when people around them use God's name as a swearword and discuss why they respond that way. Then gather their opinions on **why they think this commandment is broken so often on TV and the movies** and **how someone from another religion would feel if the name of their god was used this way.**

Allocate two people to read the two verses and write down how the Bible talks about God's name.

> **Psalm 113:1-3** – The Lord's name is one that should be praised.

> **Philippians 2:9-11** – His name is above every name and one day everyone will bow their knee to him.

Living like a Christian

Ask the young people to share their answers for the two questions: **What do people think about God when they see his people (Christians) behave badly? What does it do to his name?** Many people disregard the Christian message when those who represent it are hypocrites.

When we call ourselves Christians, we represent God to those around us through the things we say and the things we do. Read the two passages from 1 Peter and then answer: **What effect can our actions have on how people feel about God?** Both passages indicate that our good behaviour will be a witness to Christ and that the accusations of unbelievers will be silenced.

What would you say to someone who...

Based on today's study ask the young people to come up with their own advice to the four scenarios. Then summarise today's study with the question: **Why is it important to not misuse God's name?**

Two key points to keep in mind is that God's name is holy and is to be treated as such and that we are God's ambassadors with our lives and we must take that role seriously in the way we live.

Finish by suggesting ways we can help each other not to misuse God's name.

Pray: that we can live lives that show the world the greatness of God's name.

The 10 Commandments
Misusing God's name

Share: What is your full name and is there any significance to any of your names (e.g. you are named after a family member etc.)

Commandment 3 – Do not misuse God's name
How many names can you think of that the Bible uses for God? (e.g. the Lord, the Father)

_____

Read Exodus 20:7 Write this commandment in your own words:

_____

Complete the sentence: "Whenever my friends say 'oh my God' or 'Jesus Christ' as a swear word I ...

☐ Give them a dirty look   ☐ Tell them they are going to hell   ☐ Ignore it

☐ Tell them they shouldn't   ☐ Do the same thing   ☐ Other? _____

• **Why do you think this commandment is broken so often on TV and the movies?**

• **How would someone from another religion feel if the name of their god was used this way?**

God's name is treated as very special in the Bible. Read the following verses and see how the Bible talks about God's name.

Psalm 113:1-3 _____

Philippians 2:9-11 _____

Living like a Christian
The third commandment is not just about the words we say, it is also about how we represent God to other people. • **What do people think about God when they see his people (Christians) behave badly? What does it do to his name?**

When we call ourselves Christians, we represent God to those around us through the things we say and the things we do. Read the following verses: 1 Peter 2:11-12 and 1 Peter 3:15-16.

• **What effect can our actions have on how people feel about God?**

What would you say to someone who...

...says they are a Christian but uses God's name as a swear word?

...is not a Christian but uses God's name as a swear word?

...is a Christian but has a reputation of treating others badly?

...says they are a Christian but they are not (and doesn't do anything to show they might be Christian such as go to church, pray, take the Bible seriously etc)?

• **Why is it important to not misuse God's name?**

• **How can we help each other not to misuse his name?**

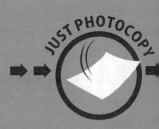

Leader's Notes
Remember the Sabbath

Aim To understand what the Bible teaches about the Sabbath (day of rest) and to evaluate whether we are living in a way that enables us to take a Sabbath.

Optional Quick Quiz: Try to remember all 10 commandments in order.
Optional exercise: See page 70
Share: Ask each person in the group what they like to do when they have some spare time. Read and discuss the scenario and ask volunteers to share their thoughts on the two questions.

Commandment 4 – Remember the Sabbath

Ask one person to read Exodus 20:8-11 and then ask each person to write out this commandment in their own words and then share their answers. **How were God's people to keep the Sabbath?** (verse 10) It was to be a day dedicated to God and a day of rest from regular daily duties/work. The rest was for every person and their animals. **What reason does God give for having a day of rest?** (verse 11) This is the pattern set by God himself when he created the world. He blessed the seventh day and made it a special day. **Why is it good to take a day off? What are the benefits?** Have the young people share their opinions here. Prepare some of your own answers in advance. Here are a few suggestions: you are more productive the other six days with a day off; you have a day to meet with God's people; you can recharge spiritually; you can rest your body and your mind; to realise that you are not indispensable. Have the young people choose items on the list that prevent them from having a day off to spend with God and his people and then discuss their answers. **How do you think you should spend your Sabbath? (What should we do with our day of rest?)** Have the young people share their ideas. Everyone likes to rest differently. Some like to do active things and some like to do nothing at all. As Christians meeting with God's people is one of our priorities for our Sabbath.

NOTE: Sabbath means Saturday in Greek. Christians celebrate the Sabbath on Sunday because it was the day of the week when Jesus rose to life though some Christians still meet on a Saturday. Some people insist that you must have a Sabbath on a particular day of the week. Colossians 2:16 teaches that we are not to allow people to judge us by which day we have as a Sabbath. While Sunday is a traditional day for the Sabbath it is not possible for everyone to choose this day. Some people have to work on a Sunday (for example doctors) and have to take a different day off. Regardless we need to work our schedules around meeting with God's people so that Bible study, youth group, church etc come first.

The Sabbath in the New Testament

Ask one or two volunteers to read Matthew 12:9-14. What had become the problem with the Sabbath at the time of Jesus? (verses 11-12) The Sabbath had become a rule where no one could do anything including helping others and doing good. **Ask for some volunteers to read Hebrews 3:12-19. What happened to the people who received the 10 commandments and why?** They failed to enter the land because of their rebellion and unbelief. For your own preparation read Numbers 14. **Ask for some volunteers to read Hebrews 4:1-11. What is the future 'Sabbath rest'?** (verses 9-11) Heaven. See also Revelation 14:13 and 21:3-4. **What warnings/instructions do these passages give us to make sure we don't make the same mistake and miss out on entering the Sabbath rest (heaven)?** We must not harden our hearts to God's Word. The remedy to this is to keep meeting with God's people (Hebrews 3:12-14. Also Hebrews 10:23-25). Finish the study by re-evaluating the advice you would give to Andrew in the scenario at the start of the study and discuss what each person needs to re-evaluate in their own lives in response to this study.

Pray for each other that we can prioritise a Sabbath day of rest each week and make meeting with God's people a priority. Pray that we won't harden our hearts to God's Word. If you have time read Matthew 11:28-30. Jesus is the only way to enter God's 'rest' (heaven).

The 10 Commandments
Remember the Sabbath

Share: When you have spare time, what do you like to do?

Scenario: *Andrew really wants to come to youth group. However, he is so busy. He has a pile of never ending schoolwork. His exams are on their way. He also has music practice and his sporting team. Basically his life is full 24/7. He has decided to skip church and youth group until he has more time.*

> **What would you tell Andrew he needs to do?**
>
> **Can you relate to his situation?**

Commandment 4 – Remember the Sabbath

The Sabbath was the day of the week that God's people Israel set aside to rest from all their work.

Read Exodus 20:8-11 Write this commandment in your own words:

_____

• **How were God's people to keep the Sabbath?** (verse 10)

• **What reason does God give for having a day of rest?** (verse 11)

• **Why is it good to take a day off? What are the benefits?**

Which of the following things might keep you from having a day off to spend time with God and his people? Choose as many as you like and then discuss your answers.

☐ Sport   ☐ Schoolwork   ☐ Work   ☐ Family commitments

☐ Friends   ☐ Social life   ☐ Hobbies   ☐ Other? _____

• **How do you think you should spend your Sabbath? (What should we do with our day of rest?)**

The Sabbath in the New Testament

At the time of Jesus (about 1800 years after the 10 commandments were written) God's people still kept the Sabbath, but they forgot the real purpose of the Sabbath. **Read Matthew 12:9-14 What had become the problem with the Sabbath at the time of Jesus?** (verses 11-12)

The 10 commandments were laws God gave to his people Israel for life in the promised land (Israel). The land represented rest for the people. **Read: Hebrews 3:12-19. What happened to the people who received the 10 commandments and why?**

The example of the disobedience of God's people serves as a warning for us today.

• **Read Hebrews 4:1-11. What is the future 'Sabbath rest'?** (verses 9-11)

• **What warnings/instructions do these passages give us to make sure we don't make the same mistake and miss out on entering the Sabbath rest (heaven)?** (Hebrews 3:12-14 and 4:1, 7 and 11)

• **What does the 4th commandment have to say to Andrew (see the beginning of the study) and to all of us in a similar situation?**

• **What do you need to change/do differently in response to what the Bible teaches about the Sabbath?**

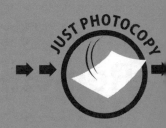

Leader's Notes
Honour your parents

Aim To understand that God has given us parents for our good and that he requires us to obey them.

Optional Quick Quiz: Try to remember all 10 commandments in order.

Optional exercise: See page 70

Ask the young people to **rate their relationship with their parent/s** by choosing one of the five boxes then discuss their answers. Then answer the questions for the two scenarios. It is important to be sensitive in a topic like this one as some young people come from painful home situations. In the first book of *Studies 2 Go* the topic 'Coping with Parents' will have raised more opportunities for discussion about these areas. The exercise in this study of rating their relationship with their parents will be an important time for discussion if there are deeper issues that need to be dealt with so be mindful to take extra time here if needed. Emphasise the fact that the rest of the study will be talking about God's ideal for parents.

Commandment 5 – Honour your parents

Ask one person to read **Exodus 20:12** and one person to read **Ephesians 6:1-3** then ask each person to write this commandment in their own words and then share their answers.

Ask the young people to volunteer their answers to the questions: **What is the hardest thing about obeying your parents? What is the best thing about obeying your parents?** You may wish to make your own list and be prepared to share it.

Why do you think honouring your parents is so important to God? The discussion around the two scenarios should give the group some good ideas about how to answer this question. A key idea is that God has chosen the pattern of parents and families to take care of us and guide us. The next passage will answer this question further. NOTE: The latter half of the 10 commandments is about our relationships with one another. God wants us to have good relationships.

Ask a volunteer to read **Proverbs 6:20-23.**

How does listening to your parents help you? Their instruction will guide you and help you to make good decisions.

Share examples of times **when it is hard to listen to what your parents tell you.**

God hates it when we disobey our parents. **Read 2 Timothy 3:1-5.**

Does it surprise you that God treats disobeying your parents as a serious offence? (Why/why not?) Ask the young people to express their thoughts about the fact that disobedience is listed with serious sins. Most people don't see disobeying parents as a very serious thing but clearly God considers it as very serious.

Read Colossians 3:20.

What is the motivation of a Christian person to obey his/her parents? It pleases the Lord.

Have the young people give themselves a score out of 10 with each of the items listed for how they can show their obedience to their parents. Share answers and then have each young person either choose the item with the lowest score and work on that this week, or think of a way they can show their parents they honour them this week.

Pray: For each other's different situations with parents and that we can be obedient.

The 10 Commandments
Honour your parents

How do you rate your relationship with your parent/s?

☐ Awesome- couldn't be better!
☐ Ok, but could be better.
☐ Pretty good - better than average.

☐ Moderate disaster - I don't understand them and they keep giving me a hard time.
☐ Total disaster - We never get along

Discuss the following scenarios...

Scenario 1: Your parents decide not to teach you anything or tell you what to do. What sort of person would you be like? What would this say to you about how much they cared for you?

Scenario 2: You don't have any parents to obey. What would it be like to grow up without any guidance?

Commandment 5 – Honour your parents

Read Exodus 20:12 and Ephesians 6:1-3 Write this commandment in your own words:

• **What is the hardest thing about obeying your parents?**

• **What is the best thing about obeying your parents?**

• **Why do you think honouring your parents is so important to God?**

Read Proverbs 6:20-23
• **How does listening to your parents help you?**

Read 2 Timothy 3:1-5
It is clear that God hates it when we disobey our parents. Notice the serious sins listed with disobeying your parents.
• **Does it surprise you that God treats disobeying your parents as a serious offence? (Why/why not?)**

Read Colossians 3:20
• **What is the motivation of a Christian person to obey his/her parents?**

Below are some ways that a young person can show that they honour their parents. Give yourself a mark out of 10 for each statement by circling the number that best describes you.
(1 = I never do this and 10 = I always do this). When you are finished discuss your answers.

I listen to my parents' advice	1 2 3 4 5 6 7 8 9 10
I ask my parents' permission for what I do	1 2 3 4 5 6 7 8 9 10
I try not to argue with my parents	1 2 3 4 5 6 7 8 9 10
I do what I am asked to do straight away	1 2 3 4 5 6 7 8 9 10
I tell my parents the truth	1 2 3 4 5 6 7 8 9 10
I speak to my parents respectfully	1 2 3 4 5 6 7 8 9 10

Choose the statement that had the lowest score and try to improve your score this week. **OR** Think about what you can do this week to show your parents that you honour them.

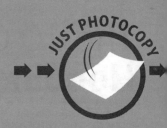

Leader's Notes
Do not murder

Aim (To know what murder is and understand that we are all capable of feelings of murder when we hate someone in our heart.

Optional Quick Quiz: Try to remember all 10 commandments in order.

Optional exercise: See page 71

What do you believe about murder? Ask the young people to circle 'True' or 'False' for the statements then discuss their answers. The answers will be revealed as the study progresses. Note that the third statement may be able to be answered either 'True' or 'False' with some qualification.

Commandment 6 – Do not murder

Ask one person to read Exodus 20:13 then ask each person to write this commandment in their own words and then share their answers.

Which of the following would you call murder? (Ask the young people to circle Yes, No OR Unsure to indicate what they believe to be murder then share answers). Below are the answers. (You don't need to look up the Bible passages unless needed.) Paying someone to kill someone else **YES** (Deuteronomy 27:25); Accidentally killing someone **NO** (Deuteronomy 19:4-6); Strongly hating someone **YES** (Matthew 5:21-22 – this will be discussed in the study); A soldier killing another soldier in war NO (Ecclesiastes 3:3) Both Jesus and John the Baptist don't acknowledge this as an issue when dealing with soldiers (Matthew 8:5-10 and Luke 3:14); Killing a person in self defence **NO** This killing is not premeditated (Deuteronomy 19:4-6); Wishing someone was dead **YES** (Matthew 5:21-22); Attacking someone so violently that they die **YES** (Numbers 35:21).

As a group, look up each passage one at a time and ask for volunteers to read each one. Collectively work out what it teaches us about murder. **Matthew 5:21-22** Hating our brother (a term used for a fellow Christian) is like murder. **James 4:1-2** Murder originates with our jealousy and selfish desires. **1 John 3:11-15** This passage combines both answers from the first two verses – jealousy leads to hatred which is murder. (Two other passages that talks of hatred in 1 John are 2:9-11 and 4:20.)

Have the young people answer the question: **What can make us hate someone?** The previous passages talk about jealousy and selfishness. Try to find some specific examples. **What are we told to do with the people we do not like?** See Luke 6:27-31 and Romans 12:17-21. We are to love them and treat them with kindness even when they treat us badly. Do to others as you would want them to do to you. Don't take revenge but overcome evil with good. **After reading what the Bible teaches about murder how would you respond to the first statement in this study ('Everyone is capable of committing murder')?** The Bible shows us that we are all capable of murder because we are all capable of hatred.

Forgiveness

The fact that the Bible was written by people who were murderers who received forgiveness shows us that while it is a serious sin it can be forgiven. It shows the depth of God's forgiveness. (You do not need to read the Bible verses about these people, they are there as references only.) **How is it possible for God to forgive a murderer?** 1 Timothy 1:15-16 teaches us that forgiveness is through Jesus. Revisit the statement at the start of the study ('**God does not forgive people who commit murder**') and ask for a second response in light of today's study. Note that he forgave Moses, David and Paul. **What does this teach you about God's forgiveness for you?** If God can forgive murder, then he can forgive us for other sin. God's forgiveness is greater than we can imagine.

Pray for each other for the ability to forgive those for whom we feel hatred. That we can forgive others as Christ forgives us and we can have love for one another. *This week: read the famous Psalm written by King David after he was found guilty of adultery and murder. Psalm 51*

The 10 Commandments
Do not murder

What do you believe about murder? Circle 'True' or 'False' for the following statements and discuss your answers.

Everyone is capable of committing murder	True	False
God does not forgive people who commit murder	True	False
People who murder others deserve to be punished severely	True	False
Murder is probably the worst thing anyone could ever do	True	False

Commandment 6 – Do not murder

Read Exodus 20:13 Write this commandment in your own words:

_____

Which of the following would you call murder?

(Circle Yes, No, or Unsure to indicate what you believe to be murder then share your answers)

Paying someone to kill someone else	Yes	No	Unsure
Accidentally killing someone	Yes	No	Unsure
Strongly hating someone	Yes	No	Unsure
A soldier killing another soldier in war	Yes	No	Unsure
Killing a person in self defence	Yes	No	Unsure
Wishing someone was dead	Yes	No	Unsure
Attacking someone so violently that they die	Yes	No	Unsure

Read the following verses. What do they teach us about murder?

Matthew 5:21-22 _____

James 4:1-2 _____

1 John 3:11-15 _____

In the New Testament murder is strongly linked to hatred. • **What can make us hate someone?**

• **What are we told to do with the people we do not like?** See Luke 6:27-31 and Romans 12:17-21

• **After reading what the Bible teaches about murder how would you respond to the first statement in this study ('Everyone is capable of committing murder')?**

Forgiveness

Did you know that large sections of the Bible were written by murderers? (Moses (Exodus 2:11-12), King David (2 Samuel 12:1-14) and The Apostle Paul (Saul) (Acts 8:3 and 9:1-2)). All three men are known as people of great faith. **What does this teach you about God's forgiveness?**

• **How is it possible for God to forgive a murderer?** (Hint: see what one of the people listed above (Paul) says about forgiveness in 1 Timothy 1:15-16)

• **How would you now respond to the second statement in this study ('God does not forgive people who commit murder')?**

• **What does this teach you about God's forgiveness for you?**

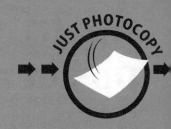

Leader's Notes
Do not commit adultery

Aim (To understand that faithfulness in marriage is God's ideal. The young people will also examine how they can set good patterns in their relationships now before they are married. NOTE: group members with divorced parents that have committed adultery may struggle with this issue. The study will help them see that such sin is forgivable.

Optional Quick Quiz: Try to remember all 10 commandments in order.

What makes a happy marriage? Ask the young people to circle up to three things from the list below then discuss their answers.

Commandment 7 – Do not commit adultery

Ask one person to read Exodus 20:14 then ask each person to write this commandment in their own words and then share their answers. At this point you may need to define adultery (unfaithfulness in marriage). The following exercise will help clarify the specifics.

What is adultery? Ask the young people to tick every box for the statements that describe what it means to commit adultery then discuss their answers. Adultery is having sex when one or both people are married to someone else. Sex between two single people is still a sin but not adultery. Adultery is described as unfaithfulness and so can be extended to intimacy that is reserved only for marriage (such as a married person kissing someone who is not their partner).

How does adultery damage a marriage relationship? The main idea is that it breaks trust. Remember that the latter half of the 10 commandments is about our relationships with one another. God wants us to have good relationships. Adultery becomes a grounds for divorce bringing a permanent end to a marriage.

Optional exercise: See page 71

Jesus teaches on adultery

Ask a volunteer to read Matthew 5:27-30 What does Jesus describe as adultery? (verse 28) He broadens adultery to looking lustfully at another person.

Adultery is unfaithfulness in marriage. **Why do you think Jesus includes looking lustfully at someone else as adultery? (How is that unfaithful?)** Like all sin it begins with an attitude of the heart.

How seriously does Jesus take adultery? (verses 29-30) It is something that can lead you to eternal destruction.

What is Jesus saying in verses 29 and 30? How can you do this (without hurting yourself!) You have to remove the sin from your life and not give in to temptation. In the case of adultery you must cut off all contact with that person.

Ask the young people to answer yes or no to the question: **Can adultery be forgiven?** Then ask one or two volunteers to read John 8:1-11. **What does this story tell you about Jesus?** Jesus extends forgiveness to the person caught in adultery. He also requires that she 'sin no more' (verse 11).

What about those who are not married?

Using the Yes/No questions discuss with the young people how they can begin setting good patterns in their relationships right now.

What can we learn from this commandment? God treats adultery seriously and his ideal for marriage is one of faithfulness.

Pray that you will treat relationships seriously and that you can have the attitude Jesus has to adultery and not the attitude of the world.

The 10 Commandments
Do not commit adultery

What makes a happy marriage?
Circle up to three things from the list below and share your answers.

Spending time together	Talking to each other	Giving gifts
Physical attraction	Saying nice things to each other	Praying together
Kindness	Being faithful to each other	Forgiving each other
Good looking partner	Sharing the money	Patience

Commandment 7 – Do not commit adultery

Read Exodus 20:14 Write this commandment in your own words:

_____

What is adultery? Tick the box of every statement that you think describes what it means to commit adultery then discuss your answers.

☐ Having sex with someone who is married when you are single
☐ Having sex with someone who is single while you are married
☐ Flirting with someone when you are going out with (dating) someone else
☐ Having sex with the person you are going out with (dating)
☐ A married person flirting with someone they are not married to
☐ Having 'an affair'
☐ A married person having an affair with someone of the same sex
☐ Being friends with someone of the opposite sex when you are married

• **How does adultery damage a marriage relationship?**

Jesus teaches on adultery

Read Matthew 5:27-30 • What does Jesus describe as adultery? (verse 28)

Adultery is unfaithfulness in marriage. • **Why do you think Jesus includes looking lustfully at someone else as adultery? (How is that unfaithful?)**

• **How seriously does Jesus take adultery?** (verses 29-30)

• **What is Jesus saying in verses 29 and 30? How can you do this (without hurting yourself!)**

• **Can adultery be forgiven? Yes/No**
  - **What does this story tell you about Jesus?**

What about those who are not married?

You might think this commandment has nothing to say to the single person, however, while you are single you need to think about setting a pattern for good relationships.

Would you flirt with someone while you are dating someone else?	Yes	No
Is your attitude to marriage that it is a lifelong promise?	Yes	No
Do you treat the opposite sex with respect?	Yes	No
Are you a faithful friend in all of your relationships?	Yes	No

• **What can we learn from this commandment?**

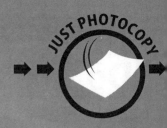
Leader's Notes
Do not steal

Aim (**To define stealing. To have the group examine their own attitude to stealing and determine whether they need to alter their actions.** NOTE: In the case of CDs and DVDs, in some countries websites are set up to download music 'legally' without paying for it. This doesn't mean it is right. In some countries child labour and prostitution is legal. In some situations what is legal may still be morally wrong according to God.

Optional Quick Quiz: Try to remember all 10 commandments in order.

Optional exercise: See page 71

Ask everyone to complete the sentence with one of the three answers provided. Encourage them to answer honestly. Be prepared that someone might share a time when they were actually caught and reported to the police. **Have you ever had anything stolen from you? What was it? How did you feel?** Share experiences. This question is to personalise stealing and realise that it affects people.

Commandment 8 – Do not steal

Ask one person to read Exodus 20:15 then ask each person to write this commandment in their own words and then share their answers.

Ask people to choose a response to the six situations to decide what they believe is stealing then share answers. All of them can be a form of stealing except keeping a gift that was stolen - that is condoning stealing. Wasting time at work is a little more vague but highlights your responsibility to do what you are paid to do.

Read the two **True Stories** then discuss what the group feels are the right responses for John and Jane. Ask them to give advice and work out what they think God wants them to do.

Do you think there is any difference between what John has done and what Jane has done? Discuss the opinions of the group but note that while Jane's actions were riskier than John's the end result was the same – they have both stolen the property.

Ask a volunteer to read 1 Corinthians 6:9-11
Why do you think God hates stealing so much? Remember that the latter half of the 10 commandments is about our relationships and stealing is anti-relationship.

Why should the Christian person not steal? (verse 11) Stealing is serious and is not the action of a Christian person who has been forgiven and changed by Christ.

Ask a volunteer to read Ephesians 4:28. Instead of stealing, work to earn their money and then share with others.

Ask a volunteer to read Galatians 6:1-2. What does this tell us to do? To help each other with sin, but be careful that we don't get tempted by the same sin.

John and Jane revisited...
What would you tell each of them to do? Make suggestions for how they can break the habit of stealing and what to do with the stolen material. Suggest that John deletes stolen songs and that Jane return the stolen property or pay for what she took.

What should you do if you own something that you know is stolen? Challenge the young people to take the same actions they advise to John and Jane if they have stolen property.

Pray that we will not be tempted to steal and that we will correct past mistakes.

The 10 Commandments
Do not steal

Complete the following sentence by ticking one of the answers:

'In regards to stealing, I...'

☐ have never stolen anything ☐ stole something once but never again ☐ steal every now and then

- **Have you ever had anything stolen from you? What was it? How did you feel?**

Commandment 8 – Do not steal

Read Exodus 20:15 Write this commandment in your own words:

_____

Look at the list below and work out which actions are stealing.

	Yes	No	Maybe
Riding the public transport without a ticket	☐	☐	☐
Keeping a gift that was given to you that you know was stolen	☐	☐	☐
Wasting time at work	☐	☐	☐
Not returning a library book	☐	☐	☐
Copying computer games or CDs	☐	☐	☐
Lying about your age to get cheaper tickets	☐	☐	☐

✦ **True Stories**

John doesn't have a lot of money but he loves music. He realises that if he copies his friends' CDs he can have all the music he wants for free.

While shopping with friends, Jane joined them in stealing some CDs. When her parents asked her where they came from she told them they were gifts.

- **What should John and Jane do? How would you advise them?**

- **What do you think God wants them to do?**

- **Do you think there is any difference between what John has done and what Jane has done?**

Read 1 Corinthians 6:9-11 We know God hates stealing. Notice the serious sins listed with stealing.
- **Why do you think he hates stealing so much?**

- **What is this passage trying to teach us?**

- **Why should the Christian person not steal?** (verse 11)

Read Ephesians 4:28
What should the thief be doing instead of stealing? _____ and _____

Read Galatians 6:1-2. • What does this tell us to do?

John and Jane revisited... _John and Jane have spent time with their Bible study groups. They realise that what they have done is wrong and wonder what they should do with their stolen material._ **What would you tell each of them to do?**

- **What should you do if you own something that you know is stolen?**

Leader's Notes
Do not give false testimony

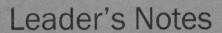

Aim) **To understand that telling lies about someone else is destructive and goes against God's standard.**

Optional Quick Quiz: Try to remember all 10 commandments in order.

Optional exercise: See page 71

Ask everyone to complete the sentence about lying with one of the five answers provided then share whether each person **finds it easy or difficult to tell the truth including when is it easy and when is it difficult.** Be prepared to discuss any issues that might arise from this exercise.

Commandment 9 – Do not give false testimony

Ask one person to read Exodus 20:16 then ask each person to write this commandment in their own words and then share their answers.

What does it mean to give false testimony? False testimony is giving false information to bring harm to someone else so that they are treated unfairly. See Isaiah 29:21.

Giving false testimony is often in the context of a witness giving evidence in a court case. **What reasons would someone have to give false testimony?** Have the group think of reasons for false testimony. Some examples are: selfish gain in some way, revenge, jealousy.

Ask for three volunteers to read the three proverbs then discuss what they say about giving false testimony:

> Proverbs 12:22 – God hates lies but loves the truth
>
> Proverbs 19:5 – A false witness will be punished
>
> Proverbs 26:28 – The person who lies hates those they hurt and their mouth brings ruin

Being truthful with one another

Ask a volunteer to read Colossians 3:9-10. **What reason does this passage give for why we should not lie to our Christian brothers/sisters?** We are to put off the old self and live righteous, holy lives that are demonstrated by our truthfulness with one another. **What does lying do to relationships?** It breaks trust. It can break friendships. It often brings hurt. **How do you feel when someone lies to you? How do you feel when someone tells lies about you?** Have the group share their personal feelings about these two questions. Ask everyone to choose from the list their response to **someone in this group telling lies about someone else in the group.** This exercise is to help the group think through how to respond to false testimony. It might be good for you as the leader to talk through how you would want to deal with this kind of situation. A helpful thing to do is to sit down with the person who is lying and to ask them to apologise. Ask the person who has been wronged to forgive them.

God, Satan and lies

Read the following verses and work out what they teach us about God, Satan and lies:

> 1. God and lies: read Titus 1:2 God cannot lie
>
> 2. Satan and lies: read John 8:44 Lying is the native tongue of Satan.

How important should the truth be to someone who is a Christian? Why? If we want to be like God and not Satan in our words we must tell the truth. Remember that the latter half of the 10 commandments is about our relationships and lying is anti-relationship.

Pray that we can be truthful with our words and so deal honestly with one another.

The 10 Commandments
Do not give false testimony

Complete the following sentence by ticking one of the answers:

'I tell lies...'

☐ All the time!

☐ Only when I'm caught doing something wrong

☐ If I need to protect my friends

☐ To get out of something I don't want to do

☐ Me? I've never lied in my life!

• **Do you find it easy or difficult to tell the truth? (When is it easy and when is it difficult?)**

Commandment 9 – Do not give false testimony

Read Exodus 20:16 Write this commandment in your own words:

_____

• **What does it mean to give false testimony?**

Giving false testimony is often in the context of a witness giving evidence in a court case.

• **What reasons would someone have to give false testimony?**

• **Look at the following proverbs and discuss what they teach about giving false testimony:**

Proverbs 12:22 _____

Proverbs 19:5 _____

Proverbs 26:28 _____

Being truthful with one another

Read Colossians 3:9-10

• **What reason does this passage give for why we should not lie to our Christian brothers/sisters?**

• **What does lying do to relationships?**

• **How do you feel when someone lies to you?**

• **How do you feel when someone tells lies about you?**

What would you do if you found that someone in this group was telling lies about someone else in the group? Choose from the list below and then discuss your answers.

☐ Nothing, I hate conflict

☐ Talk to the person spreading lies

☐ Get the whole group to talk it through

☐ Ignore them

☐ Get the group to take sides with each person

☐ Write an email to tell them to stop

☐ Tell the leader

☐ Other? _____

God, Satan and lies

Read the following verses and work out what they teach us about God, Satan and lies:

1. **God and lies: read Titus 1:2** _____

2. **Satan and lies: read John 8:44** _____

• **How important should the truth be to someone who is a Christian? Why?**

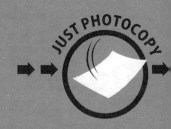

Leader's Notes
Do not covet

Aim) To understand what it means to covet and why it is wrong.

Optional Quick Quiz: Try to remember all 10 commandments in order.

Optional exercise: See page 72

Read the definition for 'covet' and make sure everyone understands. Then have each person choose from the list what they are most likely to covet of someone else then share your answers. This exercise will introduce the idea of coveting.

Commandment 10 – Do not covet

Ask one person to read Exodus 20:17 then ask each person to write this commandment in their own words and then share their answers.

Why is it wrong to covet/want what belongs to someone else? Remember that the latter half of the 10 commandments is about our relationships and coveting is anti-relationship. God does not want us to covet but to be content with what we have.

What are some negative results of jealousy of others? (How do jealous people behave?) Coveting/ jealousy leads to unhelpful actions and attitudes towards the other person and can lead to stealing and in extreme cases, hatred and murder.

Ask the young people to share how they view greed and greedy people with the questions: **How do you feel when you see a really greedy person? Do you want to be like them?**

Ask three volunteers to read the three verses that give a solution to coveting and then summarise what they teach us. The solution to coveting what others have is to learn to be content with what you have and to trust God in all circumstances.

Have a look at the five situations and think about what you would say to each one. If you don't have a great deal of time you could choose one or two that you feel are most relevant to your group.

Can you think of something that you can do in order to be more content with what you have? Make some suggestions to each other of how to deal with coveting. Some examples are: learn to be thankful for what you have – think through each good thing God has given you and thank him for each thing (do this regularly); identify those things that you tend to covet the most and work out how to avoid those temptations; memorise some of the Bible passages from this study on contentment; ask friends to keep you accountable.

Summary of the 10 Commandments

Read the summary paragraph about the 10 Commandments. Then look at the two verses that summarise the 10 commandments. **How does loving God and loving each other help us keep the 10 commandments? (For example how would your love for God and others stop you from coveting or stealing or murdering?)** When we love God we want to live thankful lives that please him. When we love a person we don't want to harm them but want to do what is best for them. Remember the conclusion to study 1: that the law demonstrated that we are sinful by outlining what sin is. It is Jesus that makes us right with God. John 1:17 – the law came through Moses, grace came through Jesus

Pray: Thank God for Jesus who brings us forgiveness for our inability to live perfect lives. Ask God to help you live lives that put God first, others second and ourselves last.

The 10 Commandments
Do not covet

Review: Try to remember all of the 10 commandments in order

Definition: To covet means to want something really badly that belongs to someone else.
Another word for coveting is jealousy.

What are you most likely to covet about someone else? Choose from the following list something you would be jealous of someone for:

☐ Physical appearance   ☐ Clothes   ☐ Family   ☐ Friends

☐ Academic achievement   ☐ Personality   ☐ Sporting ability   ☐ Other_____

Commandment 10 – Do not covet

Read Exodus 20:17 Write this commandment in your own words:

_____

• **Why is it wrong to covet/want what belongs to someone else?**

• **What are some negative results of jealousy of others? (How do jealous people behave?)**

Greed is also a form of covetousness.
• **How do you feel when you see a really greedy person? Do you want to be like them?**

• **How do you stop being jealous of what others have?**
   Read the following verses then write down the solution to overcoming jealousy (coveting).

   1 Timothy 6:6-10   Philippians 4:10-13   Hebrews 13:5

The solution to coveting what others have is _____

> **What would you say to people who behave in the following ways?**
> … I cover my jealousy of others by boasting about what I can do or what I own
> … I go into a lot of debt so I can have everything I want
> … I am tempted to covet when I see things I want at the shopping mall
> … When I see something I want I ask my parents over and over until they get it for me
> … When I am jealous of someone I speak badly of them to others

• **Can you think of something that you can do in order to be more content with what you have?**

Summary of the 10 Commandments

When we read the laws God gave his people in the 10 commandments we see that we are unable to live a perfect life that pleases God – we can't even keep 10 laws! However, God sent Jesus to die on the cross as a sacrifice for our disobedience. The Christian person obeys God because of what Jesus has done for them.

Read the following verses that sum up the commandments as loving God and loving each other.

   Matthew 22:36-40 _____

   Romans 13:8-10 _____

• **How does loving God and loving each other help us keep the 10 commandments? (For example how would your love for God and others stop you from coveting or stealing or murdering?)**

Who is Jesus?

The 'I am' sayings in John's Gospel

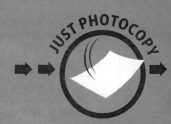

Leader's Notes
'I am the bread of life'

Aim ⎰ This study introduces the theme of the 'I am' sayings of Jesus in the book of John. It focuses on the first 'I am' saying of Jesus where he calls himself the bread of life. This study demonstrates the strong connection between Jesus and the Father and how God sent Jesus to deal with our greatest hunger of knowing God and having eternal life.

For your preparation: The 'I am' statements of Jesus have strong links with statements in the Old Testament about God. You may find it helpful to read Exodus 1-3 and 16 as preparation for this study. Note the parallels between the John and the Exodus accounts including the theme of bread from heaven and grumbling by the Jews. **Optional exercise:** See page 72

Share: The sharing question is a fun way of introducing the theme about the bread of life.

The book of John

Read aloud the short introduction to the book of John then have everyone look up **John 20:30-31** and ask for one volunteer to read it. Ask everyone to complete the statement about why John wrote the book and then have volunteers share their answers. **John wrote this book because:** he wanted us to believe that Jesus is the Christ and have life through him. *Note: When we say Jesus is the 'Christ' we are saying that he is the promised one. The word 'Christ' is not Jesus' surname but a title describing who he is.* Read the introduction to the theme of the 'I am' sayings of Jesus and then ask the young people to write three statements about themselves and then ask everyone to share their answers. Read the short introduction about the words 'I am' and then ask a volunteer to read **Exodus 3:12-15**.

I am the bread of life

Read John 6:25-59. This is a long passage! Ask for a few volunteers to read the passage. Crowds had been following Jesus and in John 6:1-15 Jesus miraculously fed 5000 with only five loaves and two fish. They continued to follow him because he had fed them once and perhaps hoped he would do it again (verse 25-26). **How would you describe the crowds who were following Jesus using verses 25-35?** Ask the young people to give their impression of the crowds. Something to note is that they had seen Jesus perform a miraculous sign by feeding the 5000 and yet they asked for another sign (verse 30). They seemed to be following Jesus for what they could get out of it. **What claims does Jesus make in verses 35-59?** Have the young people complete the sentences in their own words. They can work alone, in pairs or as a large group. Then discuss their answers. **Verse 35** – Those who come to Jesus will never *be hungry or thirsty.* **Verse 44** – For those who come to God, *Jesus will raise them to life on the last day.* See also verse 39. **Verse 45** – Everyone who listens to God will *come to Jesus.* **Verse 46** – The only one who has seen God *is the one who came down from heaven.* See also verse 38. **Verse 47-59** – Whoever eats the bread of life (i.e. has faith in Jesus) will *not die but have eternal life.* Note: eating Jesus' flesh and drinking his blood is not a literal statement. It is referring to accepting him as the bread from heaven that God gives to us to obtain eternal life (verse 47). Ask a few volunteers to read the story of Moses and the bread from heaven in Exodus 16:1-5 and 11-15. **How is the bread of life that Jesus offers different to the bread provided for Israel in the desert?** (John 6:48-51) The bread provided for Israel only satisfied for a short while – it didn't keep them alive forever. Jesus promises eternal life to those who accept him (eat the bread of life). **What do people 'hunger' for in this life?** Ask the young people to rate each of the items listed from 1 to 3 and discuss the answers. **What is our greatest need in life?** (See verses 47-51) Eternal life. **How can you avoid the temptation to chase after things that don't satisfy?** Have the young people work out some practical ways to avoid putting their trust in things that don't satisfy. **What is Jesus teaching us about himself when he says 'I am the bread of life?'** Have the young people summarise what they have learned about Jesus. Some key points are that he has revealed himself as God and is also the one who satisfies our hunger with eternal life. **Pray** for each other that we can trust in Jesus and not turn to other things to satisfy us. **Memory verse:** Work on memorising John 20:30-31 now if you have time or ask the young people to try this week. For fun ways to learn the memory verse see page 78. These ideas come from the book *Creative Christian ideas for youth groups* by Ken Moser.

Who is Jesus?
'I am the bread of life'

Share: What do you like to eat when you are really hungry?

The book of John

The book of John is the story of the life of Jesus. The book is named after the author John, who was one of Jesus' disciples. Look at the following verses and explain why John wrote this book.
Read John 20:30-31. John wrote this book because:

In the Gospel of John, Jesus teaches us who he is by making several statements about himself that all start with the words 'I am'. When we say the words 'I am' we are telling others something about ourselves. For example 'I am tired', 'I am tall', 'I am crazy'.

• **Write three simple things you can say about yourself and then share your answers.**

      I am... _____

        I am... _____

          I am... _____

The words 'I am' were important words for the Jewish people. In Exodus God revealed his name to Moses as 'I am' more than 1200 years before Jesus was born. **Read Exodus 3:12-15.**

I am the bread of life

Read John 6:25-59. How would you describe the crowds who were following Jesus using verses 25-35?

• **What claims does Jesus make to the crowds in verses 35-59?** (Complete the sentences below).

    Verse 35 Those who come to Jesus will never _____

    Verse 44 For those who come to God, Jesus will _____

    Verse 45 Everyone who listens to God will _____

    Verse 46 The only one who has seen God is _____

    Verses 47-59 Whoever eats the bread of life (i.e. has faith in Jesus) will _____

Jesus refers to a story about Moses and bread from heaven (verses 30-34 and 58). Read the story in **Exodus 16:1-5 and 11-15.**

• **How is the bread of life that Jesus offers different to the bread provided for Israel in the desert?** (John 6:48-51)

What do people 'hunger' for in this life? Rate each of the items listed below from 1 to 3 (1 = really hunger for this, 2 = sometimes hunger for this, 3 = never hunger for this), then discuss your answers.

___ Happiness   ___ Love   ___ Health   ___ Intelligence   ___ Power

___ Security   ___ Success   ___ Answers to their questions   ___ Money

___ Popularity   ___ A happy family   ___ Other_____

• **What is our greatest need in life?** (See verses 47-51)

• **How can you avoid the temptation to chase after things that don't satisfy?**

• **What is Jesus teaching us about himself when he says 'I am the bread of life?'**

Memory verse:

Try to memorise John 20:30-31. Consider this verse as we look at the statements of Jesus and try to learn it by the end of this series.

Leader's Notes
'I am the light of the world'

JUST PHOTOCOPY

Aim (To know that Jesus can give us understanding of who God is (he is the light that illuminates the truth) and through him we can have life.

Optional Quick Quiz: A helpful way to start each study is to begin with a review quiz. See page 66 74

Review Homework: Review the memory verse John 20:30-31 (see page 78 for ideas).

Optional exercise: See page 72

Share: Have the young people share something they have always wanted to see. Answers can be in regard to a place, an event, an action etc.

Jesus heals a blind man

John tells a story of a healing that illustrates Jesus' claim to be the light of the world.

Ask for volunteers to read John 9:1-34 (be prepared this is a long passage!)

What facts do we know about the blind man from this passage? He was blind from birth (verse 1-2), his blindness was not a result of his sin or his parents' sin (verse 3), he used to beg to survive (verse 8).

In pairs or on their own, have the young people write one word to describe each set of people in the story and then ask for volunteers to explain their answers.

What does the story of the healing of the blind man tell us about Jesus? (See John 9:30-33) Jesus was sent by God and God listens to him (grants his requests).

Spiritual blindness

Ask a volunteer to read John 9:35-41.

How does the healed man respond to Jesus? (verse 38) He believes and worships him.

Jesus describes the Pharisees as 'blind' (verse 41). **Read John 12:37-46. How are they blind?** They are religious leaders and know the truth but refuse to believe in Jesus. Those who believe in Jesus are no longer in darkness. The Pharisees refused to believe so they remained in spiritual darkness.

Ask the young people to give a definition of spiritual blindness in their own words. Then discuss the reasons why people refuse to believe in Jesus. They can give an alternative reason to the first three listed by filling in their own reason with the last option 'Other...'. Finish this exercise by asking the young people to suggest responses they would give to the statements. You might like to prepare you own responses in advance.

Ask for a volunteer to read John 8:12.

What is Jesus teaching about himself when he says 'I am the light of the world?' He is the light by which truth and falsehood are distinguished. He shows us the way to God.

What do you think it means to 'walk in darkness?' Ask the young people to give their thoughts. The metaphor of darkness refers to not knowing (seeing) the truth but also walking in sin (John 3:19).

What is the promise to those who believe in Jesus in John 8:12? We won't walk in darkness but will have the light of life, meaning we will know the truth about God and have eternal life.

What are some areas in your life where you need the light of Jesus to keep you from the darkness? Ask for volunteers to share areas in their life they need to change and then share how the group can help each other to follow Jesus and not walk in darkness.

Pray: Thank God for revealing himself in the person of Jesus. Pray for those we know who still walk in darkness.

Who is Jesus?
'I am the light of the world'

Share: What is something you have always wanted to see? (e.g. another country, a famous painting etc.)

Jesus heals a blind man

Read John 9:1-34.
• **What facts do we know about the blind man from this passage?** (verses 1-3 and 8)

Write one word to describe each set of people in the story and then explain your answers.

The Pharisees   One word to describe them would be: _____ _____

Explain: _____

_____

The parents   One word to describe them would be: _____

Explain: _____

_____

The healed man   One word to describe him would be: _____

Explain: _____

_____

What does the story of the healing of the blind man tell us about Jesus? (See John 9:30-33)

Spiritual blindness

Read John 9:35-41. • **How does the healed man respond to Jesus?** (verse 38)

Jesus describes the Pharisees as 'blind' (verse 41). **Read John 12:37-46.** • **How are they blind?**

Complete the sentence:

'*Someone who is spiritually blind is someone who:* _____'

Why do people find it hard to accept the truth about Jesus? Choose one of the following reasons and explain why you believe people think this way:

☐ They don't want Jesus to change their lives in any way.

☐ They don't think Jesus is relevant to their lives.

☐ They don't want to be told how to live their lives.

☐ Other?

• **How would you respond to each of the statements above?**

Read John 8:12.

• **What is Jesus teaching us about himself when he says 'I am the light of the world?'**

• **What do you think it means to 'walk in darkness'?**

• **What is the promise to those who believe in Jesus in John 8:12?**

• **What are some areas in your life where you need the light of Jesus to keep you from the darkness?**

• **How can you help each other to follow Jesus and not to walk in darkness?**

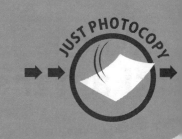

Leader's Notes
'I am the gate and the good shepherd'

Aim (To know that Jesus is the true messenger from God and to be able to identify the false teacher. Jesus puts us (the sheep) first by dying for us while false leaders put themselves first.

For your own preparation: You may find it helpful to read Ezekiel 34 and Psalm 23 as preparation for today's study. In the Old Testament God is described as a shepherd to his people (Psalm 23:1-3).

Optional Quick Quiz: See page 66

Review homework: Review the memory verse John 20:30-31 (see page 78 for ideas).

Optional exercise: See page 73

Have the young people place a □next the items on the list that they believe can teach them about God and then discuss their answers.

I am the gate

Read the introduction about false teachers and then have one or a few volunteers **read John 10:1-10**. Have the young people fill in the table either in pairs or as individuals. If your group is large enough they could break into three groups and each group could fill in the answer for one of the three titles. Ask for volunteers to share answers/show pictures. 1. **The 'robber' or 'thief'** (verses 1, 7-8, 10) refers to the one who intends to deceive and bring harm (steal, kill and destroy). Probably refers to false teachers. 2. **The 'sheep'** (verses 2-5, 8) refers to those who follow Jesus. The 'sheep' know the shepherd's voice and follow him. They won't follow a stranger. 3. **The 'gate'** (verses 2, 7-9) refers to Jesus. The 'gate' is the one through whom you can be saved. (Verses 1-10 give some confusion as the person who enters through the gate is the shepherd but the person who enters by the gate is also us. This may not come up, however, if it does, later in the study it explains the connection between the gate and the shepherd.) Ask the young people to give some examples of those who we know want to lead us away from Jesus in some way. **In what ways can they 'steal', 'kill' and 'destroy' (verse 10) the Christian?** Most false teachers want to take advantage of people for their own gain. They can exploit people for money and power among other things. Worst of all they can lead people away from Jesus so that they miss out on eternal life. **What does Jesus offer that the false teacher doesn't** (verse 10)? **What do you think this means?** Abundant life, namely eternal life in heaven. (See also Matthew 7:13-14)

I am the good shepherd

Read the introduction about the shepherd then ask for one or more volunteers to read **John 10:11-21**. NOTE: Jesus is showing us that he is God by using the title of Good Shepherd – a title used for God in the Old Testament. **What is the difference between the good shepherd and the hired hand?** The role of the shepherd is to protect the sheep but the hired hand is concerned for his own safety. (This possibly refers to the religious leaders of the day who were worried about their situation under Roman rule in Israel.) **The people listening to Jesus made two responses to him at the end of this passage, what were they?** (verse 19-21) Some said Jesus was mad and demon possessed and others said that his teachings and miracles were not those of someone demon possessed. **How do the real sheep respond to the shepherd?** (verses 3-5) They listen to the voice of Jesus and follow him. **What does the good shepherd do for his sheep?** (verse 11) Lays down his life for the sheep. Jesus does this for us when he dies on the cross (see 1 John 3:16 Note: this passage is from the letter 1 John not the Gospel of John). (His death brings forgiveness of sin so that we can have eternal life.) **What is the best way to for us to listen to the voice of the good shepherd (Jesus)? How can this group help each other not to be deceived? What can you do this week to avoid being deceived?** Ask the group for suggestions for these three questions. You might like to have your own prepared beforehand. Some important things we need to do is to meet regularly with other Christians to encourage each other and read the Bible with others as well as privately. **Pray:** thank Jesus for laying down his life for us. Pray for help to know the difference between the teachings of Jesus and a false teacher.

Who is Jesus?
'I am the gate and the good shepherd'

Indicate with a ☐which of the following you think can teach you about God then discuss your answers:

☐ Newspaper   ☐ Astrology chart   ☐ All religions   ☐ Witchcraft

☐ The Bible   ☐ My feelings   ☐ Television   ☐ Friends

☐ Family members   ☐ Creation   ☐ Church leader   ☐ Other (specify) _____

I am the gate

At the time of Jesus there were many false teachers who claimed to be sent by God to show the way to God. Jesus taught people how to recognise the true messenger of God from the false ones.

Read John 10:1-10. Using the table below, work out whom Jesus is referring to with the titles used in this passage and what he teaches you about them.

	The 'robber' or 'thief' (verses 1, 7-8, 10)	The 'sheep' (verses 2-5, 8)	The 'gate' (verses 2, 7-9)
Who does the title refer to?			
Write or draw what this passage tells you about each one.			

Give an example of someone who might want to lead the Christian person (sheep) astray. **In what ways can they 'steal', 'kill' and 'destroy' (verse 10) the Christian person?**

• What does Jesus offer that the false teacher doesn't? (verse 10) **What do you think this means?**

I am the good shepherd

When the shepherd brings the sheep into the pen at night, he lies across the doorway to keep the sheep safe. This makes him both the gate and the shepherd. **Read John 10:11-21.**
• **What is the difference between the good shepherd and the hired hand?**

The people listening to Jesus made two responses to him at the end of this passage, what were they? (verses 19-21)

    • _____

    • _____

• **How do the real sheep respond to the shepherd?** (verses 3-5)

• **What does the good shepherd do for his sheep?** (verse 11). **See also 1 John 3:16.**

• **What is the best way to for us to listen to the voice of the good shepherd (Jesus)?**

• **How can this group help each other not to be deceived?**

• **What can you do this week to avoid being deceived?**

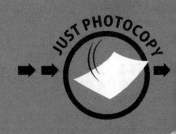

Leader's Notes
'I am the resurrection and life'

Aim (To understand that Jesus has power over death and that the Christian does not need to fear death.

For your preparation: Read Genesis 2:15-17; 3:6 and Romans 5:12; Romans 3:23 and 6:23 Hebrews 9:27, John 5:24, Acts 2:22-24.

Optional Quick Quiz: See page 67 81 75

Review homework: Review the memory verse John 20:30-31 (see page 78 for ideas).

Optional exercise: See page 73 81

Share: Have the young people share views they have heard about what happens to you after you die. This is about the opinions of others – they don't need to give their own opinion until the next exercise.

Complete the sentence: Have the young people complete the three sentences. Either ask them to write down their answers and then volunteer to share their answers OR have them share verbally. These are big issues so be prepared to spend some time on their answers if they are eager to discuss.

The death of Lazarus

Read John 11:1-37 This is a long passage so ask for volunteers and divide up the passage among them. **How did Jesus feel about Lazarus and his two sisters?** (verses 3, 5, 35-36) He loved them. **If Jesus knew that Lazarus was dying, why didn't he rush to heal his friend?** (verses 4 and 14-15) Jesus' plan was that God would be glorified through a miracle so people would believe in him. **What did Mary and Martha think Jesus could do for them?** (verses 21-22 and 32) They believed that Jesus could have prevented his death. Martha believes he still can do anything (verse 22) but she is concerned when Jesus asks to move the tomb stone away (verse 39).

Have the young people circle true or false for the three statements and then discuss their opinions. Be prepared to spend time discussing their thoughts. Have the young people choose from the list up to three ways people respond to God when tragic things happen. Discuss the answers and then ask volunteers to answer the question: **How do you respond to God when things go wrong?**

Jesus overcomes death

Read John 11:38-44 Ask for one or more volunteers to read the end of the story. **Why does Jesus pray aloud?** (verse 41-42) They would see Jesus raise Lazarus and as a result know that God had sent him because God had answered his prayer.

Read John 11:45-46 and 57 and discuss the response of those who had seen the miracle but didn't believe. Ask the young people to share if they **know anyone who knows Jesus is true but does not follow him and why.**

Who is Jesus?

Read the short introduction. Ask a volunteer to read 1 John 5:11-13 **What assurance does this passage give those who trust in Jesus?** Those who know Jesus have eternal life and this is something we can know for certain.

What can you say to someone who fears death? Ask the young people to share their answers. A key point is that Jesus has power over death and those who believe in him need not fear death. If the person who fears death is not a Christian you should talk to them about how Jesus has destroyed death and can take away our fear.

Pray: thank God that Jesus has overcome death and that we do not need to be afraid.

Who is Jesus?
'I am the resurrection and life'

Share: What are some common views about what happens to you after you die?

Complete the sentence:

> *I personally believe that when people die they...*
>
> *When someone you know dies you feel...*
>
> *What I fear about death is...*

The death of Lazarus

Read John 11:1-37

• **How did Jesus feel about Lazarus and his two sisters?** (verses 3, 5, 35-36)

• **If Jesus knew that Lazarus was dying, why didn't he rush to heal his friend?** (verses 4 and 14-15)

• **What did Mary and Martha think Jesus could do for them?** (verses 21-22 and 32)

Circle True or False for the following statements and then explain each of your answers.

God cares when someone we love is sick or dies	True	False
It is unusual for something bad to happen to people who love God	True	False
God is in control even when things don't turn out the way we want	True	False

How do people usually respond to God when tragic things happen? Choose up to three responses from the following list and discuss your answers.

☐ They get angry with God   ☐ They think God doesn't care

☐ They refuse to believe in God   ☐ They ask God: 'why me?'

☐ They think God is weak   ☐ They think God is punishing them for something

• **How do you respond to God when things go wrong (such as the death of someone you love)?**

Jesus overcomes death

Read John 11:38-44

Jesus prays to the Father to answer his prayer for Lazarus (verse 41). **Why does Jesus pray aloud?** (verse 41-42)

Have a look at the responses to the miracle Jesus performed: read John 11:45-46 and 57.
• **Why do you think some who saw the miraculous signs Jesus performed didn't follow him?**

• **Do you know anyone who knows Jesus is true but does not follow him? (Why don't they follow Jesus?)**

Who is Jesus?

When Jesus says 'I am the resurrection and the life' in verse 25, he is teaching us that he is the only one who can conquer death. He proved this with his own death by rising from the dead.

Read 1 John 5:11-13. What assurance does this passage give those who trust in Jesus?

• **What can you say to someone who fears death?**

Leader's Notes
'I am the way and the truth and the life'

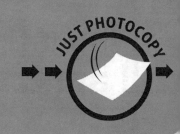

Aim To understand that Jesus is the only way to know God and that Jesus and God the Father are one.

Optional Quick Quiz: See page 67
Review Homework: Review the memory verse John 20:30-31 (see page 78 for ideas).
Optional exercise: See page 73
Share: Introduce the idea of getting to know God with a sharing question about getting to know your friends. Then ask for suggestions of some ways people get to know God. You may want to have some suggestions prepared beforehand or work through some popular religions and share what you know about how they say you get to know God. Then ask whether they believe Jesus is the only way to God with the Agree/Disagree question.

I am the way and the truth and the life

Read the short introduction and ask for some volunteers to **read John 14:1-11. What do you think Jesus is promising in verses 1-4?** There is a place in heaven for those who believe in Jesus. **How would these words bring comfort?** We can have certainty of eternal life. **What is Jesus saying in verses 6-11 about how to get to know God?** (See also John 1:18) Jesus is the only way to the Father because he is also God.

One God

Read the paragraph and look at the diagram about God being trinity. Spend some time talking through what this means. Note that this is a very difficult issue for everyone because it is a paradox that God can be one, but also three. Some things to note are: **1.** They are three distinct persons with different roles, for example Jesus dies on the cross, not the Father or the Holy Spirit, however... **2.** They are one and work as one. You may like to read some other passages from John that talk about God at work through the Spirit to prepare for today's study: John 14:15-31 and 16:5-15. **3.** There are some analogies that you can use to understand the trinity a little better. One example is marriage where two people become one or an egg is made of yolk, white and shell but all are still egg. Be careful however, since analogies only take you so far. Some examples are unhelpful such as water can be seen in different forms: liquid, steam and ice. This is unhelpful because God is not one person who changes into different forms, but God is three distinct persons who are one. **4.** Don't worry if you can't answer every question about the Trinity – that is the whole point of it being a paradox! **What are some things Jesus teaches about his relationship with the Father?** If you have seen Jesus you have seen the Father (verse 9); Jesus is in the Father and the Father is in Jesus (verse 10-11); Jesus works under the Father's authority (verse 11). In pairs, look at the five statements that summarise Jesus' words from this passage. Ask the group to share examples of situations where these statements would bring comfort to the Christian person. Ask the young people to choose the statement that brings the most comfort or encouragement in his/her Christian faith right now and explain why. This section is worth spending some time on if they have questions or doubts. **What is Jesus teaching us about himself when he says 'I am the way and the truth and the life?'** Ask the young people what they have learned about Jesus from this passage. Some key points are: God is his father, he is the only way to the Father, if you know Jesus you know the Father, he is one with the Father and he is sent from the Father. Note especially that today's passage speaks very clearly about the fact that Jesus is God. **If someone asked you 'How do you get to know God?' what would you say?** Ask the young people to give their answers. You might like to have your own answers prepared beforehand. Some important things to note are: you get to know God through Jesus. Jesus opens up the way to God through dying on the cross. You must believe in him and you must decide to follow him.

Pray: that you will continue to understand who Jesus is.

Who is Jesus?
'I am the way and the truth and the life'

Share: Name one of your friends and tell the group how you got to know them.

- **What are some ways people try to get close to God?**

'There are many ways to God; Jesus is just one of those ways.' ☐ Agree ☐ Disagree
Discuss your answer.

I am the way and the truth and the life

In the following passage, Jesus speaks words of comfort to his disciples since he knows he is about to be arrested and then killed on the cross. **Read John 14:1-11.**

- **What do you think Jesus is promising in verses 1-4?**

- **How do these words bring comfort?**

- **What is Jesus saying in verses 6-11 about how to get to know God?** (See also John 1:18)

One God

One of the hardest things to understand about Jesus is how he can be God. The Bible makes it clear that there is only one true God. However, God is revealed to be three persons: the Father, the Son (Jesus) and the Holy Spirit. The word used to describe the relationship of all three is the 'Trinity'. Have a look at the diagram below illustrating the idea of the Trinity.

- **What are some things that are hard to understand about the Trinity?**

- **What are some things Jesus teaches about his relationship with the Father?** (verses 9-11)

> Look at the following statements that summarise Jesus' words in this passage.
>
> *Jesus is coming back to take us to his father's house (verses 2-3)*
>
> *Jesus is the only way to God the Father (verse 6)*
>
> *If you know Jesus you know God the Father (verses 7-9)*
>
> *Jesus and God the Father are one (verse 10)*
>
> *Jesus' miracles prove that he is from God (verse 11)*

Give examples of situations where these statements would bring comfort to the Christian person.

Choose one that brings you the most comfort or encouragement in your Christian faith right now and explain why.

- **What is Jesus teaching us about himself when he says 'I am the way and the truth and the life?'**

- **If someone asked you 'How do you get to know God?' what would you say?**

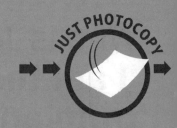

Leader's Notes
'I am the true vine'

Aim (God has chosen us to be people who live in obedience to him (produce fruit). To do this we must remain in Jesus (the vine).

Optional Quick Quiz: See page 67. **Review Homework:** Review the memory verse John 20:30-31 (see page 78 for ideas). **Optional exercise:** See page 73. **For your preparation:** God's people Israel were often referred to as a vineyard (see Isaiah 5:1-2, 7). Read what Jesus said about Israel producing fruit in Matthew 21:33-45 and Luke 3:8-9. These words were fulfilled when people who were not Israelites (Gentiles) became Christians. Other helpful passages: Romans 7:4-5, Colossians 1:10 and Galatians 5:16-26. Ask each person to answer the sharing question that introduces the theme of 'fruit'.

Bearing fruit

Ask some volunteers to read John 15:1-11. What do you think it means to produce fruit and remain in Jesus? The Christian person is to live a life that bears spiritual fruit. We need to be growing in our faith. See Galatians 5:16-26 that talks about fruit of the Spirit. There seems to be a strong connection between remaining in Jesus and obeying him. We need to show our faith through an obedient life. **What warnings does this passage give us?** The branches that don't produce fruit will be cut off (verse 2). The branches that don't remain in Jesus will be cut off and wither and be thrown into the fire (verse 6). Ask the young people to describe the person who obeys God's commands. If this is difficult ask them to identify someone they know who obeys God's commands and describe them. Some examples may be: they choose to do what is right even when it is unpopular; they are strong in their faith; they take their faith seriously; they are an example/role-model to others. Read the short introduction to the exercise and then have the young people put a cross on the line to help them evaluate the areas in their lives that might need pruning. Ask if anyone would like to share their answers and suggest **one area in their life where they feel God needs to change them. How can we help each other in the areas where we need to change?** Take suggestions on how the group can encourage each other to change. Some suggestions might be: be willing to point out weak areas; be willing to help each other overcome weak areas; be open to being accountable to each other. **How can we help each other to remain joined to the true vine (Jesus)?** Take suggestions on how the group can help each other. Some suggestions might be: urge each other to be committed to Christian fellowship; follow people up when they miss a few times or stop coming; talk to each other about spiritual things. Note: It is not our obedience that makes us friends with God. Verses 4-5 make it clear we cannot bear fruit until we are attached to the vine. Also verse 16 in the next section talks about God choosing us not the other way around. The Holy Spirit lives in the Christian and helps us to obey God. The Spirit will convict you of sin, guide you in the truth and bring glory to Jesus (John 16:5-15). He helps us to know Jesus and understand what he has done for us.

The obedient life

Ask one or more volunteers to read John 15:12-17. What kind of love are we to have for each other in verses 12-13? We are to love each other the way God has loved us. His love is a sacrificial love. He gave up his life for us. Have the young people think of some practical examples of how we can lay down our lives for each other (sacrifice for each other and put each others' needs before our own). **What is God's plan for those he chooses?** (verse 16) He chooses us to bear fruit (those things that demonstrate a godly, obedient life like the fruit of the Spirit in Galatians 5:22-26). When a person obeys the commands of Jesus and loves other Christians, Jesus says he will give them whatever they ask (verses 7 and 16). **What does this kind of person pray for?** Things that please God rather than prayers for his/her own selfish desires. Have the group write down two things they can pray for that Jesus would want them to pray for and pray for these things at the end of the study.

Who is Jesus? Ask volunteers to share at least one thing (there is space for three on the sheet) that they have learnt about Jesus from looking at the 'I am' statements in the book of John.

Who is Jesus?
'I am the true vine'

Share: If you could only eat one fruit for the rest of your life, which one would you choose?

Bearing fruit

Read John 15:1-11. • **What do you think it means to 'produce fruit' and 'remain in Jesus'?**

• **What warnings does this passage give us?** (verses 2 and 6)

Describe the person who obeys God's commands. **What are they like?**

God removes the dead wood and works in the life of the believer so that they bear good fruit. Put a cross on each line below to indicate whether you need God to change you in the areas listed.

	Time for pruning	Nothing needs to change
My thoughts	|———————————————|	
The way I speak to others	|———————————————|	
The way I treat others	|———————————————|	
My use of time	|———————————————|	
My attitude to God	|———————————————|	

• **What is one area in your life where you feel God needs to change you?**

• **How can we help each other in the areas where we need to change?**

• **How can we help each other to remain joined to the true vine (Jesus)?**

The obedient life

Read John 15:12-17

• **What kind of love are we to have for each other in verses 12-13?** (Give practical examples.)

God has chosen us. **What is God's plan for those he chooses?** (verse 16)

When a person obeys the commands of Jesus and loves other Christians, Jesus says he will give them whatever they ask (verses 7 and 16). • **What does this kind of person pray for?**

• **What are two things you can pray for that Jesus would want you to pray for?**

1._____

2._____

Who is Jesus?

• **What are some things you have learned about Jesus through the 'I am' statements in the book of John?**

Jesus is... _____

Jesus is... _____

Jesus is... _____

Spend some time praying for the two things each person listed that Jesus would want us to pray for.

Practical Christian Living

Studies in the letter of James

Leader's Notes
Dealing with tough times

Aim (This study will introduce the book of James as a book of advice on how to live as a Christian. It will also show the young person how the Christian can deal with tough times.

These studies will not cover the whole book of James. The passages not used are noted as further reading. Here are some options that will help you to cover the whole book:

1. Write your own studies on the passages not used. **2.** Have the young people read the passages themselves during the week. **3.** Ask for a volunteer each week to start the study time with a 2-5 minute devotion on the passages not covered.

Share: Ask each of the young people to share their answers to one or both of the questions.

The Book of James

Ask a volunteer to read James 1:1 and then another volunteer to read the short introduction.

Some other helpful information is that James was the brother of Jesus and the term 'twelve tribes' is used to refer to Israel. **Optional exercise:** See page 74

Dealing with hard times

Ask a few volunteers to read aloud James 1:2-18. **What advice does James give the Christian in this section?** Ask the young people to come up with as many pieces of advice as they can find in this section. It doesn't matter if they don't find everything. Here is a list: **Verses 2-4** – Consider the positives of suffering. **Verses 5-8** – Ask for wisdom and believe that God will give it to you. **Verses 9-11** – Be content whatever your circumstances; don't let poverty or wealth cause you to be sinful. **Verse 12** – Persevere in hard times. **Verses 13-15** – Don't blame God when you are tempted to sin but resist your sinful desires. **Based on the advice James is giving in this passage, what kind of things do you think the readers were experiencing?** Have the group try to work out what might be happening to the readers based on the advice James is giving them. Some suggestions: They are undergoing some kind of hard time; they are experiencing some issues in regards to the poor and the wealthy; they may be tempted not to persevere; they are blaming God for their temptations; they may be doubting God's goodness to them. Ask volunteers to **share a situation they found hard to deal with** and share one word that describes how they felt. Then ask the group to complete the exercise that answers the question '**what do you do when times are hard?**' and discuss the answers. Ask the young people to explain verses 2-4 in their own words. Look also at verse 12 and a similar passage Romans 5:1-5. **What do verses 5-8 tell you to do?** Ask God for wisdom and believe that he will give it to you. Ask the group to share **some examples of times when people need wisdom. Where does temptation come from according to verses 13-15?** Our own sinful desires. **How can you avoid temptation?** Have the group offer some suggestions but also guide them towards the idea that God wants us to put a stop to our wrong desires before they lead us into temptation. **Ask a volunteer to read James 1:22.** Ask the young people to complete the sentence of how they will deal with tough times (in other words how will they put this part of the Bible into practice). **How can this group be a support to each other during tough times?** Ask the young people to suggest ways they can support each other. Some suggestions are: pray for each other in this group; ask how each other are going during the week; encourage each other with what the Bible tells us to do. If you have some more time read all of James 1:19-27 and ask: **What are some things this passage tells the Christian to do?** Have the group find the instructions given to the Christian in this passage. Don't worry if they don't get every one. **Verse 19** – Quick to listen, slow to speak and slow to become angry. **Verse 20** – Get rid of wrong thinking and bad behaviour. **Verses 22-25** – Obey God's word. **Verses 26** – Keep control of your tongue. **Verse 27** – Show true religious behaviour by caring for the helpless in society. **Verse 27** – Don't be corrupted by the world. Discuss whether the young people find it hard to do what the Bible teaches and how they can be obedient even when it is hard. **Homework:** Ask the young people to follow the homework for the week. **Pray.** Share any difficulties people are facing right now and pray for each other.

Practical Christian Living - James

Practical Christian Living - James
Dealing with tough times

Share: What is some good advice you have been given? **OR** do you have some good advice you would share with others?

The Book of James
Read James 1:1
James wrote this letter to Jews who followed Jesus and were scattered out from Jerusalem after persecution had broken out. The book is a collection of advice on how they were to live as Christians

> ### Memory verse
> **Read James 1:22**
> Consider this verse as we look at the book of James and try to learn it by the end of this series.
> **What does this verse mean?**

Dealing with hard times
Read James 1:2-18

- **What advice does James give the Christian in this section?** (There is quite a lot!)

- **Based on the advice James is giving in this passage, what kind of trials do you think the readers were experiencing?**

- **What is one situation you found hard to deal with?**
  Using one word, describe how the situation made you feel.

> **What do you do when times are hard?**
> Tick the boxes that best describe how you respond to hard times and discuss your answers:
>
> | | Never | Sometimes | Mostly | Always |
> |---|---|---|---|---|
> | Get angry with God | ☐ | ☐ | ☐ | ☐ |
> | Pray | ☐ | ☐ | ☐ | ☐ |
> | Make life miserable for others | ☐ | ☐ | ☐ | ☐ |
> | Become moody | ☐ | ☐ | ☐ | ☐ |
> | Ask friends to help or pray for me | ☐ | ☐ | ☐ | ☐ |
> | Talk to someone | ☐ | ☐ | ☐ | ☐ |

Explain in your own words why the Christian is able to deal with hard times with the positive attitude described in verses 2-4. (See also verse 12 and Romans 5:1-5) **What do verses 5-8 tell you to do?**

- **What are some examples of times when people need wisdom?**

When we go through hard times, we can be tempted to disobey God and do what we feel.
- **Where does temptation come from according to verses 13-15?**

- **How can you avoid temptation?**

Advice is only valuable when we use it. **Read James 1:22.** In response to this part of the Bible (complete the sentence): When I face hard times I will...

- **How can this group be a support to each other during tough times?**

Homework: This week read James 1:19-27 and try to put into practice James 1:19.
Try also to memorise James 1:22.

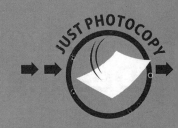
Leader's Notes
Playing favourites

Aim (This study teaches that it is wrong to show favouritism by treating people differently from others and that God does not show favouritism.

Optional Quick Quiz: A helpful way to start each study is to begin with a review quiz. See page 68

Review homework: Ask if anyone tried to do the homework of implementing James 1:19 and have them share their experience. Review the memory verse (see page 78 for ideas).

Optional exercise: See page 74

Introduce the study by having the young people write down three characteristics of people they like to spend time with and then have them share their answers. Ask volunteers to then share how they choose the friends they have.

Showing favouritism (A common word used to describe favouritism is discrimination)

Ask one or two volunteers to read aloud James 2:1-7. **What advice does James give the Christian in this section?** We are not to treat people differently because of their appearance or wealth. **Based on the advice James is giving in this passage, what were the readers doing wrong?** They showed favouritism to the wealthy and discriminated against the poor by treating some better than others. Note also that they had issues with the rich people they were showing favouritism towards who were taking them to court and saying bad things against them. **What reasons would someone have to favour a rich person over someone else?** Ask volunteers to come up with some reasons why someone may favour a rich person over others. Then look at some other **reasons why someone may be more popular than others** by circling three of the choices and then discussing the answers. Ask them to suggest some reasons why someone might favour those with the qualities they circled. **What is the problem with showing favouritism for the popular people?** (verse 4) We make ourselves the judges of who is acceptable and who isn't. (We are not to judge others by outward appearance and make distinctions.)

Treating others equally

Ask a few volunteers to read aloud James 2:8-13. **What does this passage say to someone who claims to be a keen Christian, but doesn't treat others equally?** The person who judges by outward appearance is guilty of sin. This sin is treated seriously just as other commandments are. It is no good treating some laws seriously and not others. Discuss how James 2:12-13 should influence the way we behave towards others. Since we have been set free from judgement we should not judge others by outward appearance. We should show mercy. **How does God show his mercy to us while still judging our sin?** (Hint: 2 Corinthians 5:21) God judges our sin through punishing Jesus in our place. Another helpful verse is 1 Peter 3:18. For the following two questions, ask five volunteers to read aloud the passages one by one. After each verse is read, have the young people write and share their answers before moving on to the next verse.

How does God treat those who trust in him?

    Acts 10:34-35 – God treats everyone impartially.

    Galatians 3:26-28 – All who follow Christ are equal in God's sight.

How are we to treat others?

    Leviticus 19:15 – Be honest and don't judge unfairly against the poor or favour the rich.

    Romans 12:16 – Do not be proud or think of yourself more highly than you should.

    Philippians 2:3 – Show humility and consider others as more significant than you.

Ask volunteers to suggest what they can do or change to not show favouritism and then have the group suggest ways that they can avoid showing favouritism. Two suggestions for the group is to be friendly to everyone who joins and when people get together for any reason invite everyone in the group.

Always remind the young people of James 1:22 – they must put this advice into practice.

Pray for this group that it will be accepting to all we know and not show favouritism.

More-Studies-2-go

Practical Christian Living - James
Playing favourites

Share: Describe three characteristics of the kind of people you usually like to spend time with (e.g. funny, friendly etc).

1. _____
2. _____
3. _____

How do you choose the friends you have?

Showing favouritism
Read: James 2:1-7

• What advice does James give the Christian in this section?

• Based on the advice James is giving in this passage, what were the readers doing wrong?

• What reasons would someone have to favour a rich person over someone else?

What are some other reasons why someone would be more popular than others?
(Circle your top three reasons and then discuss your answers)

Good looking	Owns great stuff	Funny	Athletic
Friendly	Kind	Generous	Important family
Wears good clothes	Intelligent	Confident	Other_____?

What is the problem with showing favouritism for the popular people? (verse 4)

Treating others equally
Read James 2:8-13.

• What does this passage say to someone who claims to be a keen Christian, but doesn't treat others equally?

• Discuss how James 2:12-13 should influence the way we behave towards others.

• How does God show his mercy to us while still judging our sin? (Hint: 2 Corinthians 5:21)

How does God treat those who trust in him?

Acts 10:34-35 _____

Galatians 3:26-28 _____

How are we to treat others?

Leviticus 19:15 _____

Romans 12:16 _____

Philippians 2:3 _____

• What is one thing you can do/change to make sure you don't show favouritism?

• How can this group be a group that does not show favouritism?

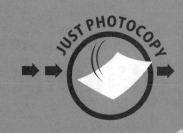

Leader's Notes
Real faith

Aim) At the end of the study the young people will understand the meaning of true faith and be encouraged to show their faith by their actions.

Optional Quick Quiz: See page 68

Memory verse Review the memory verse James 1:22 (see page 78 for ideas).

Optional exercise: See page 74

Share: Introduce the concept of faith with the sharing question and then have them write a definition for the word 'FAITH'. Discuss their answers and then compare their definition with the one given in Hebrews 11:1.

Faith and deeds

Have the young people share their opinions on whether **you can just say you are a Christian and not act like one.** This will prepare them for the Bible passage. **Ask one or a couple of young people to read James 2:14-19. What does this passage say to the person who says they believe in God but their actions don't prove it?** Their faith is not a genuine faith but a dead faith.

Discuss how the person needing help in verses 15-16 would feel if a Christian ignored their needs. Some suggestions are: they would think Christians are hypocrites or uncaring; they might become angry at Christians; they might not want to have anything to do with the Christian faith.

Two examples of people with faith

Ask for a couple of volunteers to read the story of Abraham in **Genesis 22:1-14** and then have one person read **James 2:20-24**. Discuss how they think they might feel if God asked them to give up something they love.

Ask a couple of volunteers to read the story of Rahab in **Joshua 2:1-14** and one person to read **James 2:25**. Share how we can be encouraged by the examples of faith shown by Abraham and Rahab. Note the risk that both of these people took. Think also about the definition of faith read earlier in Hebrews 11:1.

Have the young people share some things that they **might have to do because they are Christian that they would find hard to do.** You might want to have some examples ready for them.

You and your faith

Ask one person to read James 2:26 Note that the Christian person puts their faith in Jesus (John 3:16, John 20:30-31 and Romans 10:9). Ask for volunteers to answer the question about how they show that they have faith in Jesus. Discuss ways in which **they can show evidence of their faith through actions.**

There are six examples of where a young person may be able to show they have faith by what they do and how they act. Have the young people place a cross on the line that best indicates how much they are demonstrating their faith in Jesus. These are only a few examples – you may like to add some more that you think are issues for the young people in your group. After they have shared their answers ask for volunteers to share **if there are any areas they would like to improve or change.**

Always remind the young people of James 1:22 – they must put this advice into practice.

Pray: Share some ways that faith can be shown in action this week and pray for opportunities and courage to take those opportunities when they come. Pray also for friends and family who don't as yet have any faith.

Practical Christian Living - James
Real faith

Share: What are some things you have not seen but still believe they exist? (e.g. air)

Write a definition for the word 'FAITH':

_____

Read Hebrews 11:1 and compare your answer above to what the Bible says faith is.

Faith and deeds

• **Do you think you can say you are a Christian and not act like one? Why?/Why not?**

Read James 2:14-19
• **What does this passage say to the person who says they believe in God but their actions don't prove it?**

James gives an example of someone saying they have faith but not living it out in verses 15-16.
• **What would the person who needed help in this example think about the Christian faith if someone acted like that towards them?**

Two examples of people with faith
James gives two examples of faith in the Old Testament.

> ✦ **Example 1: Read the story of Abraham** in Genesis 22:1-14 and James 2:20-24.
> • **What is one thing that is important to you?**
>   **How would you feel if God asked you give that one thing up?**
>
> ✦ **Example 2: Read the story of Rahab** in Joshua 2:1-14 and James 2:25.
> • **How can we be encouraged in our own faith by the examples of Abraham and Rahab?**

• **What are some things that you might have to do because you are a Christian that you would find hard to do?**

You and your faith
Read James 2:26
• **In what ways do you show that you have faith in Jesus?**
  (How do people around you know you are a Christian?)

Below are some examples of where a person can show they have faith in Jesus by what they do. Place a cross on the line to indicate how much you are showing that you are a Christian in each area then share your answers.

	Obvious I am a Christian	No-one knows I am a Christian
How I deal with peer pressure	|_____|
The things I say	|_____|
Trusting God for my future	|_____|
How I deal with hard times	|_____|
My commitment to Christian fellowship	|_____|
How I act at home	|_____|

• **Are there any areas in your life you would like to improve or change?**

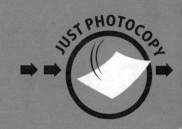

Controlling the tongue

Aim (This study challenges us about the way we use our tongues.

Optional Quick Quiz: See page 68 **Review** the memory verse James 1:22 (see page 78 for ideas). Ask if anyone was able to show their faith in their actions this week. **Optional Exercise:** See page 74
Share: Have everyone share something nice they have said or someone has said to them. Some might find this harder than others but persist in having them think of something.

Controlling the tongue Ask one or a few volunteers to read James 3:1-12. Have the young people share destructive ways they can use their words and positive ways. They can either write their own lists and then share them as a group or make their lists collectively. Some suggestions are: Positive: compliments, pointing out good things someone has said or done, reminding each other of God's promises. Negative: Gossip, backstabbing, slandering, saying petty or jealous things, swearing.

The Tongue is like...	How is the tongue like this image?
1. The bit for a horse's mouth (verse 3)	Verse 3: It can control our whole body
2. Rudder of a ship (verse 4)	Verse 5: It is small but can make great boasts
3. Small spark/fire (verse 5)	Verse 5: It can do great damage
4. Fire (verse 6)	Verse 6: It can spread evil though our whole life

This section begins with a warning to those who want to be leaders (verse 1). **What can happen when a leader uses their tongue to teach false things?** Have the young people think of how a false teacher can do damage. Here are some suggestions: They can have great influence over people to do or believe the wrong thing; they teach people to believe false things; they can lead people away from the truth.
Ask one or two volunteers to **read Matthew 7:15-23. How can we know if someone is a false teacher?** Their behaviour will show us what they truly believe (see especially verses 18 and 21). It is important to note that people might even do things that seem amazing (verse 22) but we still need to test the fruit of their lives.

The power of words Ask three volunteers to each read one of the verses from Proverbs. After each one is read have the group try to explain what they mean and then write down the agreed answers. The answers below are a guideline. Many of the Proverbs here are straightforward.
Proverbs 12:18 – Thoughtless words can hurt but kind words can heal
Proverbs 15:4 – Kind words lift you up but harsh words make you feel down
Proverbs 18:21 – Your words can hurt or help so be careful what you say

Why must we be careful about how we use our tongue? Our words can really hurt people and do damage. Have the group give each other advice on practical ways in which they can avoid misusing their tongue in the five ways listed. You don't have to read the Bible verses listed. Write down the answers in the group advice section. Below are some suggested answers.

Group Advice: To avoid gossiping I need to...(Gossip involves saying things that are awful about someone who is not present.) Some ways to avoid this are: Don't spread information about other people when it is unhelpful; don't spread information about others when you know they wouldn't want you to; don't participate in gossip when others speak it. **To avoid swearing I need to...**(Swearing is using words that are crude and usually offensive. It is often a habit). Some ways to avoid this are: Ask friends to point out words that you currently use that you want to stop using. Think of alternative words to express yourself. **To avoid lying to people I need to...**Be honest! Don't put yourself in situations where you are tempted to lie. **To avoid slandering people I need to...**This one is similar to gossip. One suggestion is to try to see the good side of others. **To avoid boasting I need to...**Don't be arrogant. Don't seek your importance from the opinions of others. Finish this section by asking volunteers to share **which of the 5 problems listed they need to work on the most and how your Christian friends can help you**

The Christian must be different! As a volunteer to read James 3:9-12 Why must the Christian be different in the way we use our tongue? We are hypocrites when we use our words to praise God and then hurt others. We must be consistent with what we say. Encourage everyone to do the further reading during the week. **Pray:** Share some areas in your life that need to change in light of today's study and pray for each other.

Practical Christian Living - James
Controlling the tongue

Share: What is one nice thing someone has said to you or that you have said to someone?

Controlling the tongue

Read James 3:1-12. Give examples of some destructive ways we can use our words (e.g. gossip):

Give examples of some positive ways we can use our words (e.g. compliment):

James 3:3-6 gives us four images (illustrations/examples) of what the tongue is like. Have a look at the four images below and work out why our tongues can be like these.

The Tongue is like...	How is the tongue like this image?
1. The bit for a horse's mouth (verse 3)	Verse 3 _____
2. Rudder of a ship (verse 4)	Verse 5 _____
3. Small spark (verse 5)	Verse 5 _____
4. Fire (verse 6)	Verse 6 _____

The warnings and instructions about controlling the tongue are important for all Christians but especially for those who want to be leaders (verse 1).
• **What can happen when a leader uses their tongue to teach false things?**

Read Matthew 7:15-23. • **How can we know if someone is a false teacher?**

The power of words

Have a look at the following verses from Proverbs about the power of our words. Read them aloud and try to explain what they mean.

Proverbs 12:18 _____

Proverbs 15:4 _____

Proverbs 18:21 _____

• **Why must we be careful about how we use our tongue?**

Below is a list of five ways the Bible tells us not to misuse our tongue. As a group, work out practical ways to avoid doing these things.

Problem:	Group Advice:
Gossip (Proverbs 16:28)	To avoid gossiping I need to...
Swearing (Ephesians 4:29)	To avoid swearing I need to...
Lying (Colossians 3:9-10)	To avoid lying to people I need...
Slander (saying false things to damage someone's reputation) James 4:11	To avoid slandering people I need to...
Boasting (James 4:13-18)	To avoid boasting I need to...

• **Which one of these do you need to work on the most?**

• **How can your Christian friends help you?**

The Christian must be different!

See James 3:9-12. • **Why must the Christian be different in the way we use our tongue?**

Further reading: James 3:13-18. Think about what this passage teaches about true wisdom.

Friendship with the world vs friendship with God

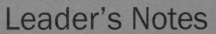

Aim (To understand the temptation and danger for the Christian to love the world. Friendship with the world leads us away from God and causes tension with each other. The solution is to submit our lives to God and put him first.

Optional Quick Quiz: See page 69

Review the memory verse James 1:22 (see page 78 for ideas). Ask if anyone did the further reading (James 3:13-18) and ask, 'what do you think it says about true wisdom?'

Optional Exercise: See page 74

Share: Ask each of the young people to answer the sharing question.

Our struggle with the world

Ask for one or more volunteers to read James 4:1-12. Based on what James is teaching in this passage, what were the readers doing wrong? They were fighting with each other; they were jealous of each other, they wanted things for their own pleasure; they didn't care about their sin; they were judging each other unfairly or unmercifully. **What is the reason James gives for fights and quarrels?** (verses 1-2) Jealousy and selfishness. James refers to killing in verse 2 which is synonymous with hate (See Matthew 5:21-22 and 1 John 3:15). People covet and fight rather than pray. **Why doesn't God let us have our own way?** (verses 2-3) They are not trusting God through prayer and when they do pray they ask for selfish things. What do these passages teach us about how the Christian is to live in relation to the world? Ask three volunteers to read aloud the passages one by one. After each verse is read, have the young people write and share their answers before moving on to the next verse.

Matthew 6:24 – You cannot love both God and money.

1 Timothy 6:6-10 – We must be satisfied with what we have and not desire more.

1 John 2:15-17 – Do not love what the world offers as it is passing away.

At this point in the study make sure everyone understands what it means to love the world. Based on the Bible passages so far it is: living for your own desires; loving the temporary things that the world offers; being discontent with what we already have. Verse 4 refers to these kinds of people as adulterous – they have two choices – to love God or love the world and they are choosing to be spiritually unfaithful. This makes God jealous for our love (verse 5). Have the young people choose something from the list that they could be tempted to love more than God and/or could draw them away from Christian fellowship and share their answers. Note that some of these things are not bad but when they take over our priorities they can be harmful to our faith. **How can love of these things hinder your relationship with God and/or your relationship with other Christians?** Have the young people offer suggestions. An obvious problem comes when something prevents you from meeting regularly with your Christian group e.g. sport or study instead of Bible study, youth group or church.

Dealing with our struggle

Have each person quietly or in pairs find all the instructions James gives in verses 7-10 to help us get our priorities straight and stop loving the world. Share your answers. **How can following these instructions help us to stop loving the world?** It helps us acknowledge our sinfulness and self-centredness and focus our attention back on obeying God and asking for his help. Note: these instructions are to be done NOW. **When is a time we might NOT feel bad about loving the world?** Think of examples of when we sin but don't feel bad. Often this happens when we do things that we don't think are wrong or we are being disobedient and don't want to change our lifestyle. Ask the young people to suggest ways they **can help each other** not to be wilfully sinful. Encourage everyone to do the further reading during the week.

Pray: For each other that you can say 'no' to your selfish desires and live in obedience to God.

Practical Christian Living - James

Practical Christian Living - James
Friendship with the world
vs friendship with God

Share: What is something you have envied in someone else? (For example, you want to be like them in some way or you want to have something they own).

Our struggle with the world

Read James 4:1-12

• **Based on what James is teaching in this passage, what were the readers doing wrong?**

• **What is the reason James gives for fights and quarrels?** (verses 1-2)

• **Why doesn't God let us have our own way?** (verses 2-3)

James summarises the cause of these problems as 'friendship with the world' (verse 4). Look at the following verses and work out what they teach us about how the Christian is to live in relation to the world:

Matthew 6:24 _____

1 Timothy 6:6-10 _____

1 John 2:15-17 _____

> Look at the list below and try to work out the areas in your life where you are tempted to love what the world offers. Choose the one that you think could become a greater priority than your relationship with God or fellowship with other Christians then discuss your answers.
>
> ☐ Popularity   ☐ Opposite sex   ☐ Parties   ☐ Owning lots of stuff   ☐ Success
> ☐ Internet   ☐ Music   ☐ Desire for fame   ☐ Physical appearance   ☐ Sport
> ☐ Money   ☐ Drugs   ☐ Feeling important   ☐ Academic achievement
> ☐ Other _____

• **How can love of these things hinder your relationship with God and/or your relationship with other Christians?**

Dealing with our struggle

James gives a list of instructions in verses 7-10 to help us get our priorities straight and stop loving the world. Underline every instruction you find in this passage printed below.

> *7 Submit yourselves, then, to God. Resist the devil, and he will flee from you. 8 Come near to God and he will come near to you. Wash your hands, you sinners, and purify your hearts, you double-minded. 9 Grieve, mourn and wail. Change your laughter to mourning and your joy to gloom. 10 Humble yourselves before the Lord, and he will lift you up.* (NIV Translation)

• **How can following these instructions help us to stop loving the world?**

This passage urges us to stop being arrogant and feel bad about our sin (verses 8-9).
• **When is a time we might NOT feel bad about loving the world?**

• **How can we help each other in this area?**

Further reading: Look at James 4:11-12 and then read Matthew 7:1-5 and work out what these passages teach us about the way we are to deal with each other. Read James 4:13-17 and work out what it is teaching us about trusting God in all areas of our lives.

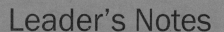
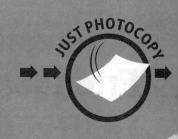

Leader's Notes
Faithfulness to God in all circumstances

Aim (To understand that suffering is a part of the Christian life and we need to respond to it with faithfulness and trust in God.

Optional Quick Quiz: See page 69 **Review the memory verse** James 1:22 (see page 78 for ideas). Ask if anyone did the further reading (James 4:11-12, Matthew 7:1-5 and James 4:13-17) and share what they learned.

Optional exercise: See page 75

Share: Have the young people think about how they respond when things don't go their way through the sharing question and the list of examples.

Patience in suffering

Ask two volunteers to read James 5:1-12

What are the people in verses 1-6 being accused of? (What kind of lives did they live?) They put their trust in wealth and oppressed the poor.

What judgement do they face because of their way of life? Their wealth will be taken from them and the Lord will avenge those they oppressed.

How are the people in verses 7-12 different from the first group? (What was happening in their lives?) They have not lived lives of luxury and have suffered. They may even be the people whom the first group oppressed.

What are some examples of how we suffer for being Christians? Have the young people give examples of suffering as Christians in their own context.

What instructions does this passage give us about what to do when we suffer? Be patient and wait for the Lord's return. Continue to be faithful in your behaviour (don't start grumbling) and remain steadfast.

Work through the passages and exercise regarding the two examples of the prophets and Job noting how they suffered and how they responded to suffering. Have the young people talk about how they would personally respond to the same kinds of experiences with the question: **Do you think you could respond to hardship the way the prophets and Job did? Why/why not?**

Verse 12 talks about making oaths. This verse reminds us of Matthew 5:33-37 which talks about making promises that you don't keep. It is like making a promise but crossing your fingers behind your back thinking that this means you are not bound to your promise. With this section you can choose to answer the question: **How does being an honest person show your faithfulness to God in all circumstances? Can you think of a circumstance when you would be tempted to lie?** Or you can comment on the verse and skip to the next section about prayer since this idea might be a little complicated.

Responding in prayer

Ask one or more volunteers to read James 5:13-20

Use this section as a prayer time by sharing names that fit the descriptions from this passage and praying for them as a group. Make sure you share prayer points of thanks especially in light of what was learned about the response of the prophets to hardship (Matthew 5:11-12).

Practical Christian Living - James

Practical Christian Living - James
Faithfulness to God in all circumstances

Share: a time when things didn't happen the way you wanted them to.

What do you do when things don't go your way? Choose one of the following examples and then share your answers.

☐ Throw a tantrum ☐ Argue ☐ Get angry ☐ Accept it
☐ Cry ☐ Go into a mood ☐ Slam doors ☐ Make life hard for everyone else
☐ Complain ☐ Other_____

Patience in suffering
Read James 5:1-12.

• What are the people in verses 1-6 being accused of? (What kind of lives did they live?)

• What judgement do they face because of their way of life?

• How are the people in verses 7-12 different from the first group? (What was happening in their lives?)

• What are some examples of how we suffer for being Christians?

• What instructions does this passage give us about what to do when we suffer?

James uses the prophets and a man called Job (pronounced Jobe) as examples to us of people who suffered with patience and stood firm in their faith (verses 10-11).
Read Matthew 5:11-12. • **What kind of suffering does Jesus tell us to expect that the Old Testament prophets also experienced?**

From the list below, what is the worst kind of suffering that you could experience? Rate in order from 1 to 5 (1 = the worst thing and 5 is the least bad thing) then discuss your answers.

___ You lose everything you own ___ Your family dies
___ The person closest to you doesn't support you ___ You become really sick
___ Your friends don't support you

Job was a man who suffered a great deal. In fact everything in the list above of things that can go wrong happened to Job! **How did Job respond when bad times came? Read Job 1:21-22.**

Do you think you could respond to hardship the way the prophets and Job did? Why/why not?

Make sure that in all circumstances you are a trustworthy person who keeps their promises (verse 12). How does being an honest person show your faithfulness to God in all circumstances? Can you think of a circumstance when you would be tempted to lie?

Responding in prayer
Read James 5:13-20.
James urges us to respond with prayer to all circumstances in life. Write down the names of people you know in the following circumstances and then pray for them as a group.

Times to pray	People you know who need prayer
When someone is in trouble (verse 13)	_____
When someone is sick (verse 14-15)	_____
When someone is wandering from their faith (verses 15-16 and 19-20)	_____

This passage also urges us to say prayers of thanks (verse 13). Think of some things that you are thankful for and pray 'thank you prayers' to God.

Topical Studies

Church • Guidance • Suicide • Family • Drugs • Satan • Easter • Busyness

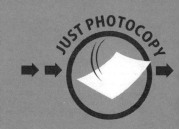

Leader's Notes
Going to church

Aim At the end of this study the young people will understand the place of church in the life of the Christian and their responsibility as a member of the church.

For your preparation: Acts 2:42-47. This passage gives us a good description of what Christians are meant to do when they meet together.

Optional exercise: See page 75

What do you make a priority on Sunday? Open the study with the exercise rating in order from 1-9 the list of activities regarding what they do on Sunday then discuss their answers. They can only use each number once (for example they can't answer with the number 1 more than once), so each of the 9 numbers should be used.

Answer the two questions about why people do and don't go to church. This will give you an understanding of what they, their friends and family think about going to church.

What is church all about?

Read the short introduction and then have a few volunteers read 1 Corinthians 12:12-27. Have the group share their impressions of church from this passage. You may like to have some of your own impressions ready. Some key points to bring out are that we need each other and that we all have a valuable role to play. Have the young people give suggestions for how they would respond to the three statements based on 1 Corinthians 12:12-27. Some suggested guidelines are: each person contributes and is needed (verses 14-20); we all need the contribution of others for our encouragement (verse 21). Look at verse 26 and explain what it means and give examples of how it works. You may like to have a few examples prepared. Some suggestions are: if someone is grieving, we all feel sadness with them; if someone receives recognition for something they have achieved, we are happy for them.

Ask a volunteer to read Hebrews 10:23-25. What does this passage tell us about the importance of meeting together as Christians? We need to meet to urge each other to love and to do good deeds (verse 24). We must not get out of the habit of meeting together (verse 25). We need to meet to encourage each other (verse 25). Ask for three volunteers to read the Bible verses. After each verse is read, write down what the Bible says about the responsibility of the members of the church.

> **1 Peter 1:22** – Love each other (see also Romans 13:8).
> **Colossians 3:13** – Forgive each other.
> **1 John 3:16-18** – Love each other practically, for example, sharing our possessions.

In what ways can you contribute to your church? Ask for volunteers to suggest ways in which they can personally contribute to the body of Christ.

Give me some advice!

This final section will identify some of the issues that the group may have with church. Ask the group to come up with advice for the three scenarios. Encourage them to see especially how they can be a help to each other in these kinds of situations.

What would you say to someone who says they follow Jesus, but does not go to church? Following Jesus is about being a part of his people (the body of Christ). It is clear from the Bible that being a part of the body is not optional but each one is to contribute to the encouragement of others. (It is a sad fact that many people who don't want to be part of the body do not grow in their faith and quite often fail to continue in their faith.) It might be helpful to also ask the young people 'what happens if we don't go to church?'

Pray for your church and for each other's commitment to it.

Going to church

What do you do on Sunday? Rate in order from 1-9 what you do in order of importance on Sunday. 1 is your highest priority (always do this) and 9 is your lowest priority (sometimes do this). When you are finished, discuss your answers.

___ Homework   ___ Family gatherings   ___ Church/Christian group

___ Sport   ___ Relaxing   ___Work

___ Seeing friends   ___ Clean my bedroom   ___ Other? _____

- **What are some reasons why people don't go to church?**

- **What are some reasons why people *do* go to church?**

What is church all about?

Church is not a building but a group of people. In the book of 1 Corinthians the church is described as a body with many parts. People who follow Jesus are members of the body.

Read 1 Corinthians 12:12-27

- **What impression do you get about the church from this passage?**

What does this passage say to someone who:

... doesn't think it matters whether they go to church?

... is jealous of the abilities of other people in the church?

... thinks they are more important or valuable than other people at church?

Explain what verse 26 means and think of some examples of how this works.

Read Hebrews 10:23-25

- **What does this passage tell us about the importance of meeting together as Christians?**

The Bible says a great deal about the responsibility of members of the church towards each other. Here are a few:

1 Peter 1:22 _____

Colossians 3:13 _____

1 John 3:16-18 _____

- **In what ways can you contribute to your church?**

Give me some advice!

What if I don't understand what goes on at church?

What if I don't know anyone at church?

What if there are people at church I don't get along with?

- **What would you say to someone who says that they follow Jesus, but does not go to church?**

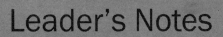

Guidance - How can I know what decisions God wants me to make?

Aim (This study will help the young people to understand some good principles in making wise decisions that please God.

Optional exercise: See page 75

Share: Have each of the young people share an important decision they have had to make. (This may be harder for a younger person.) Have everyone complete the first exercise on how they look for guidance and discuss the answers. Have everyone complete the second exercise on their decision-making and discuss the answers.

Do I put out a fleece or take a vote?

Ask four volunteers to read the four passages from Judges on the story of Gideon (Judges 6:1-6, 6:11-16 and 6:36-40 (Judges 8:28). **What did God ask Gideon to do, and what did God promise him?** (verses 14-16) God asked him to fight against the Midianites and promised that he would strike them down and save Israel. **Why do you think Gideon put out the fleece? Why were his actions disobedient?** Gideon was clearly reluctant to do what God had asked. God had told Gideon that he would be with him and give him victory and yet Gideon tested him with the fleece in order to confirm what God had already promised. **What are some things we already know God wants us to do and do not need to ask for guidance?** Ask the young people to share what they know God wants based on what the Bible tells us, for example, we are to love our neighbour as ourselves, we are not to lie etc. Ask for two volunteers to read the other Bible example of asking for guidance in Acts 1:15-17 and 21-26. **How was the decision process for Judas' replacement different from what Gideon did?** (What did they do to make the decision?) Unlike Gideon, the disciples did not have a clear request from God of which person to choose. Together they worked out who would best suit the position of the 12th disciple based on wise decisions (21-22). When they narrowed the choice to two equally valid candidates they prayed for guidance and then cast lots (like flipping a coin cf Proverbs 16:33) for God to choose. Some of the key principles in the Acts story are: talking through choices with other godly people; prayer; being willing to make a choice based on the information at hand.

Guide me!

Read the short introduction to this section. You may want to see if there are any questions or confusion about making choices. Note: Sometimes we are presented with a choice of right and wrong. In this situation you don't need guidance, you need to choose obedience over disobedience. Sometimes we are presented with two good options with no wrong choice. At this point we pray for guidance and then choose. God will open and close the right doors to lead you where he wants. Sometimes a step of faith is making your own choice. Read the following practical tips for seeking guidance and then have the group add their own suggestions to the list. Read the following verses. What do they teach us about guidance? **James 1:5-6** – God gives wisdom to those who ask for it and we must trust him to do this. **Proverbs 3:5-6** – Trust in God and not in your own understanding. Live an obedient life and he will direct you. **2 Timothy 3:16-17** – The Bible is God's Word (as clear to us as when he spoke to Gideon!) and gives us what we need for living a godly life and making godly choices. Sometimes people trust things such as visions, hunches, dreams or the level of peace they experience. These are to be treated with a great deal of caution as we can be mislead by our own wrong desires rather than trusting what we know for certain from God's Word (remember Gideon). It is important that these feelings and experiences are measured by what scripture says. They must be consistent with scripture, for example, someone may have real peace about dating a non-Christian but that is incompatible with scripture. One other passage that is helpful to keep in mind when making choices is **Romans 8:28** – God is always working for your good, even when sometimes it might not feel like it. **Pray.** Share some things that people currently need guidance for and then pray. Pray also for other needs in your group.

Guidance - How can I know what decisions God wants me to make?

Share: What is an important decision you have had to make?

'When I need guidance I...'

Choose as many of the following boxes that match your answer.

☐ Pray ☐ Read the Bible ☐ Go with my feelings
☐ Speak with my parents ☐ Speak with older Christians ☐ Talk to my friends
☐ Flip a coin ☐ Consult my horoscope ☐ Other_____

Put a cross on the lines below in the place that best describes you and discuss your answers.

	Yes that's me	No not me at all
I find it hard to make decisions	|————————————————————|
I worry that I make decisions that God doesn't like	|————————————————————|
I try to make the kind of decisions God wants me to	|————————————————————|
I never have important decisions to make	|————————————————————|

Do I put out a fleece or take a vote?

Read the following selections of the story about a man called Gideon who asked God for guidance. Judges 6:1-6 and 6:11-16 and 6:36-40. (The final outcome: Judges 8:28)

• **What did God ask Gideon to do, and what did God promise him?** (verses 14-16)

• **Why do you think Gideon put out the fleece? Why were his actions disobedient?**

• **What are some things we already know God wants us to do and do not need to ask for guidance?**

Another example from the Bible where some people sought guidance from God was in the choosing a replacement for Judas. Judas was one of Jesus' 12 disciples who betrayed Jesus and then killed himself. Read Acts 1:15-17 and 21-26. **How was the decision process for Judas' replacement different from what Gideon did?** (What did they do to make the decision?)

Guide me!

Sometimes there are no right and wrong answers and we just have to make a decision from one of two good options, such as the example of the choosing of Judas' replacement. Read the following practical tips for seeking guidance and then add some of your own suggestions to the list.

Pray about your decision
Speak to older, wiser Christians
Sit down and think through all the options and then choose
Ask, 'Does the Bible have any specific teaching on the issue to help guide me?'

If you have time read what the following verses teach us about guidance:

James 1:5-6 _____

Proverbs 3:5-6 _____

2 Timothy 3:16-17 _____

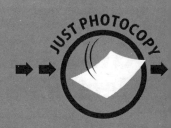

Leader's Notes
Suicide

Aim (This study will help the young people to see that suicide is not the option for the Christian person and to recognise alternatives for dealing with tough times. (This study may be helpful in dealing with a suicide of someone known to the group but is also for prevention.)

Note: Use this study to work out where the people in your group are at, especially noting how they handle their problems and if they have people around them who can support them. Be prepared for people to feel sad if they have had a friend or relative commit suicide. For your preparation: Do some reading about youth suicide. Also read Hebrews 12:1-13 and Romans 8:28-39. A word of caution: This topic is very sensitive but is necessary to discuss due to the high rate of suicide among teenagers. You may like to ask a trained counsellor to join you to talk about this topic (especially if there has been a suicide that people in the group are aware of). On a theological note: Suicide does not mean that a person automatically goes to hell. It is not the unforgivable sin. A person goes to hell for rejecting Jesus as Lord. There are many sins we commit that we never think to ask forgiveness for but Jesus still forgives us. Sometimes people who are Christians have suffered terrible depression and committed suicide – what they did was wrong but Jesus can still forgive them.

Optional exercise: See page 75

Share: Have each person share one good thing they have to live for. If the group is older and it is appropriate you could ask if people have ever known someone who has committed suicide. Have each person number 1-3 the top three reasons why people commit suicide and discuss the answers. Have the young people share what they feel is difficult for families and friends of those who commit suicide and whether they would feel different if the death had occurred for other reasons. Note: Many people feel a sense of guilt over the suicide of a loved one as they wonder if they could have prevented it.

God is there for you!

Read the short introduction to this section and then look at the Bible passages. Write next to each verse what the passage says to the person going through a tough time. **Hebrews 12:7-11** – Endure hardship like loving discipline from God who works to bring about holiness in our lives. **Hebrews 13:5-6** – God will never leave us and so we can be unafraid of the future. **From these verses, why is suicide the wrong option for someone who follows Jesus?** We all face hardship however we know that God is at work in our lives for good. Suicide is giving up our trust that God is in control.

Christian community

Read the short introduction to this section and write down what each verse below says to us about how the Christian family helps us in tough times. **2 Corinthians 1:3-4** – The Christian community comforts each other in our troubles. **Galatians 6:2** – The Christian community is to carry each other's burdens. Have the young people identify from the list the good suggestions for dealing with tough times. Correct answers are: talk to someone; ask God to help you; read the Bible; talk to a counsellor; ask friends to pray for you; tell your close friends; meet with Christians for support. Note: what is needed is a combination of these answers. **What should you do if you suspect someone you know is thinking about suicide?** Ask the young people for their suggestions but be prepared with some of your own. Some helpful advice is: never promise to keep a secret if you don't know what it is – if someone tells you they want to commit suicide that is not a secret you can keep; talk with them and be their friend; take them to an adult that can help them. **What is one thing you would want to say to someone who is contemplating suicide?** Ask the young people to share their answer. Try to draw on parts of the Bible from today's study. Ask the young people to offer solutions to the number of reasons for suicide they chose from the list at the beginning of this study. Then have each person name two people they could talk to in tough times. If anyone cannot name a person they could speak with, talk with them after the study and let them know that you could be one of those people.

Further reading: Ask the young people to read Psalm 23 this week.

Suicide

Share: What is one good thing you have to live for?

Choose the main 3 reasons from the list below why you think people consider suicide as an option. Order them from 1-3 with 1 being the top reason. Discuss your answers.

___ Loneliness   ___ They feel useless   ___ It seems the only solution to a problem

___ Depression   ___ They have lost hope   ___ They feel no-one cares

___ Family issues   ___ Parents divorcing   ___ They have broken up with a partner

___ They have been hurt   ___ They have made a mistake   ___ Other_____

- **Why is suicide so difficult for the friends and family that are left behind?**

- **Would the family and friends feel differently if the person who committed suicide had died through illness or in a car accident?**

God is there for you!

When things are tough, the Bible assures us that God is with us and that he understands and cares about our situations. Read the following passages from Hebrews and work out what they say to us when we face tough times. • **What does this mean in tough times?**

Hebrews 12:7-11 _____

Hebrews 13:5-6 _____

- **From these verses, why is suicide the wrong option for someone who follows Jesus?**

Christian community

When Jesus calls you to follow him, he also calls you into a family of others who follow him. The Christian family is a place of support and encouragement. Read the following passages and work out what they say to us about how the Christian family helps us in tough times. • **What does this mean in tough times?**

2 Corinthians 1:3-4 _____

Galatians 6:2 _____

Below are some suggestions of what to do when you are going through a tough time. Put a tick next to the good suggestions and a cross next to the bad suggestions and discuss your answers.

☐ Talk to someone   ☐ Ask God to help you   ☐ Try to act happy

☐ Read the Bible   ☐ Talk to a counsellor   ☐ Ask friends to pray for you

☐ Pretend everything is OK   ☐ Tell your close friends   ☐ Meet with Christians for support

- **What should you do if you suspect someone you know is thinking about suicide?**

- **What is one thing you would want to say to someone who is contemplating suicide?**

Look again at the exercise at the beginning of the study. Using the option you rated Number 1, give an answer/solution to the problem other than suicide.

Name two people you feel you could talk to if you needed help in tough times.

Further Reading: Psalm 23

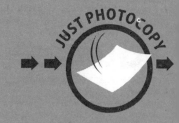

Leader's Notes
Coping with family

Aim This study will help the young people to discuss the areas that cause them difficulty within their family. It will also help them to see the responsibility they have to their family and the importance of their own Christian witness at home. This study will help you, the leader, get a better picture of home life for the individuals in your group.

Optional exercise: See page 76

Ask each of the young people to complete the sentence.

From the list of family members ask each person to indicate how well they get along with each one and share their answers. Some young people may not have all the relatives listed (for example not all young people have a dad who is a part of their lives or may have had grandparents die).

Have the young people share the answers to the three questions about whom they get along with the best from their family and, what they imagine their own family in the future will be like, compared to the one they in now.

Have the young people indicate which members of their family are Christians. Be prepared that most young people will want to believe their family members are Christian even when they are not. Do not worry about that at this time but just accept their answers.

Have each person share **if being a Christian (or others in the family being Christian) makes a difference to family relationships.**

What teaching does the Bible give us about families?

Ask a volunteer to read the bible passage and write what instruction it gives us about families.

1 Timothy 5:3-4 and 8 We have a responsibility to provide for our immediate family, especially those who are more dependent. This is putting our religion into practice. This pleases God. To refuse this responsibility is to deny the faith.

Jesus and his family

It is helpful for the young people to realise that if their family does not get along, this is a common experience. Even Jesus didn't experience harmony with his family all the time. Read the short introduction about Jesus and his family and ask two volunteers to read the two passages.

How can the example of Jesus be an encouragement to us? Have the young people share how they are encouraged by Jesus' example. Each person may be encouraged in different ways by Jesus' example because home life will involve different struggles for each person.

The Christian family

Read the short introduction and then ask four volunteers to read the four passages about the Christian family. For some people the knowledge of a Christian family can be a real help especially for those from broken or dysfunctional homes.

What is one thing that you can do in your own family that will make your family relationships better? Have the young people share how they can contribute to making home life better.

Pray for each other's individual home situations.

Coping with family

Complete the sentence: 'A really good thing about my family is...'

Who do you get along with the most in your family? Check the boxes that suit your answers.

	Always get along	Mostly get along	Don't really talk	Never see them	Fight
Brother/sister	☐	☐	☐	☐	☐
Mother	☐	☐	☐	☐	☐
Father	☐	☐	☐	☐	☐
Grandparent/s	☐	☐	☐	☐	☐
Aunt/s	☐	☐	☐	☐	☐
Uncle/s	☐	☐	☐	☐	☐
Other?	☐	☐	☐	☐	☐

- **Who do you get along with and why?**

- **Who do you not get along with and why?**

- **How is your current family like the one you will hope to have when you are older?**

Check boxes below of who are Christian in your family:

☐ Brother/Sister ☐ Mother ☐ Father ☐ Grandparent/s ☐ Aunt/s ☐ Uncle/s ☐ Other?

- **Does it make a difference to your family relationships that you or others are Christian?**

What teaching does the Bible give us about families?

Read the following passage and note what instruction it gives us about families:

1 Timothy 5:3-4 and 8 _____

Jesus and his family

Not all families get along all the time. Jesus understands having struggles with family. Even his own family misunderstood him. **Read Mark 3:20-21** However, when Jesus was dying on the cross, he was concerned for the welfare of his widowed mother. **Read John 19:25-27.**

- **How can the example of Jesus be an encouragement to us?**

The Christian Family

While God has given you an earthly family, he also gives you a new family when you believe and follow him. Read:

1 John 3:1   John 1:10-13   Galatians 6:10   Ephesians 2:19

- **What is one thing that you can do in your own family that will make your family relationships better?**

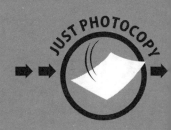

Individual Topics

Leader's Notes
Drug abuse

Aim To understand that drugs are harmful and are not compatible with the Christian life. At the end of the study the group members will know why and how to avoid temptation.

Note: This study is not dealing with drugs that are prescribed by a doctor or addictions to coffee etc. While some verses are about alcohol, the issue of getting drunk is for another study. There are times when drugs are helpful and good such as taking pain relievers after an operation or for an injury or dealing with issues such as depression. This study is focusing on taking drugs (that are often illegal) in order to numb the mind and the feelings so that a person can escape reality. For your own preparation: Read: Proverbs 20:1; Proverbs 23:20-21; Proverbs 25:28; Romans 13:13; 1 Corinthians 5:11; Galatians 5:19-23; 1 Peter 4:3-4; 2 Peter 1:3-7. **Optional exercise:** See page 76. Ask the young people to circle 'true' or 'false' to the statements and discuss their answers. **What are some reasons why people start taking drugs?** Have the young people share their opinions. Also suggest some of your own. Here are a few: experimenting; peer pressure; it is a problem in their home; they are unhappy and want to escape. **List the common illegal drugs that young people take:** Ask the young people to share the drugs they have heard of. Here are some examples: marijuana, crystal meth, cocaine, heroin, speed, ecstacy. **What do you see are the problems that come from taking drugs?** Ask the young people to share their opinions. Also suggest some of your own. Here are a few: they are not in control and hurt themselves or others; they can be taken advantage of in some way when under the influence; they can become addicted; they can sustain permanent mental and physical damage; they could die.

The Christian person is to... 1. Be clear minded and self-controlled. Read the short introduction, ask two volunteers to read the two verses and write down what they teach about self-control. **Ephesians 5:15-18** – We are to live as wise people, following the will of God and not use anything that causes a lack of self-control which prevents us from following God. (The example of the substance that leads to lack of self-control is alcohol but the principle is the same). **1 Peter 5:8** – be self-controlled and alert so you will not fall prey to your enemy Satan. Another passage that is helpful for you to know is Galatians 5:19-23. We can live according to the sinful nature which indulges in sin or by the Spirit which includes showing self-control. **2. Live as a new creation.** Ask two volunteers to read 2 Corinthians 5:17 and Ephesians 4:22-24. The section in the box is about how the Christian is to view things that are legal but morally wrong. For example it is not illegal to get drunk but the Christian person is clearly told not to. **If drugs were legal where you lived, would that make it OK to use them?** Ask the young people their opinion about taking drugs when they are legal then read **Romans 6:11-14 and 19**. Remember that the Christian person is not to lose self-control but live as a new creation. We are not to be mastered by sin and use our bodies for sinful activity.

How to avoid drugs Read the two pieces of advice for avoiding drugs. (1. Don't start and 2. Don't let others pressure you.) Another helpful passage on dealing with people who lead you astray is Mark 9:43-47. The group may like to talk about this a little before moving on. Finish this section by asking people to volunteer other ways to avoid drugs.

Helping a friend Look at the suggestions for how to help a friend struggling with drug use. Discuss them and add your own suggestions. Ask a volunteer to read Galatians 6:1. **What warning does this give us when we are helping others caught in a sin?** We are to help others who are struggling with sin but we must be careful not to end up joining them. **What can we do this week (or the next time we are tempted) in light of today's study?** Ask the young people for their suggestions and offer some of your own. Some examples are: think about who they spend time with and whether anything needs to change; go to parties etc with a group of Christian friends who will help each other to stay pure; agree to be available to each other if someone needs help to avoid temptation.

Pray for people you know who are dealing with these problems as well as other prayer concerns.

More-Studies-2-go

Drug abuse

Circle true or false for the following statements:

Most people my age have tried marijuana	True	False
I have faced pressure to take drugs	True	False
There is no harm in trying a drug once	True	False
You can take drugs regularly without it affecting your life	True	False
I personally know people who take hard drugs	True	False
People take drugs to escape reality	True	False
It is OK for a Christian to use drugs every now and then	True	False

- **People I know who use illegal drugs** (circle one): • none • a few • quite a lot • most of my friends

- **What are some reasons why people start taking drugs?**

- **List the common illegal drugs that young people take:**

- **What do you see are the problems that come from taking drugs?**

The Christian person is to...

1. Be clear minded and self-controlled. A person under the influence of drugs is not in complete control of their mind or body. When you are out of control you can't live the way God wants you to live. You think only about yourself and you are unable to be a help to others. Read what the Bible says about self-control:

Ephesians 5:15-18 _____

1 Peter 5:8 _____

2. Live as a new creation. Read 2 Corinthians 5:17 and Ephesians 4:22-24

> If drugs were legal where you lived, would that make it OK to use them?
> Read what the Bible teaches about the correct way we should use our bodies: Romans 6:11-14 & 19

How to avoid drugs

1. Don't start! Many people begin by 'experimenting' with drugs and then cannot stop.

2. Don't let others pressure you. 1 Corinthians 15:33 says Do not be misled: 'Bad company corrupts good character.' In some cases avoiding drug use may mean avoiding certain people who lead you astray.

- **What other advice would you give someone on how to avoid using drugs?**

Helping a friend

Here are some suggestions for how to help a friend struggling with drug use. Discuss them and add your own suggestions.

Help them deal with peer pressure by being another peer that helps them say 'no'
Spend time with them
Talk to them about what the Bible teaches
Speaking with an adult that could help
Other _____

Read Galatians 6:1. • **What warning does this give us when we are helping others caught in a sin?**

- **What can we do this week (or the next time we are tempted) in light of today's study?**

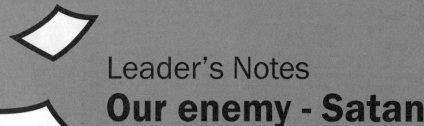

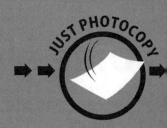

Leader's Notes
Our enemy - Satan

Aim (To understand who Satan is, how Jesus has defeated him and how we can resist his tricks.

For your own preparation: Read Job 1 and Job 2. Note in this story that Satan has to ask permission to harm Job since God is in control (Job 1:11-12; 2:3 and 2:6-7). The Bible talks of two types of people: children of God (John 1:10-13) and children of the Devil (John 8:39-47). See also 1 John 3:8 and 1 John 3:10.

Optional exercise: See page 76

Exercise: all answers are NO. It might be helpful to share their answers and wait to the end of the study to give the correct answers as a review.

Who is he and where did he come from?

Read the short introduction about Satan and then ask a volunteer to **read Genesis 3:1-5 What information does this passage give us about Satan?** He was there at the beginning of creation; He is crafty; he is created by God; he leads people to disobey God's Word. **Important note:** A common misunderstanding is that God is the ruler of heaven and Satan is the ruler of hell. However hell was prepared for the punishment of Satan and his angels, he does not rule there. Satan knows Jesus has defeated him and his last efforts are to take as many people to hell with him as he can. See Matthew 25:41.

Our enemy's strategies

Look at the following verses and work out what Satan does to work against God and his people:

> **Luke 8:12** - The devil takes away God's Word from people's hearts so they will not believe.

> **John 8:44** - He tells lies.

> **2 Corinthians 11:13-15** - He pretends to be something good and attractive.

Give specific examples of lies or tricks Satan uses to pull us away from living the way Jesus wants us to. Ask the young people to offer suggestions. Have some of your own prepared. Here are some suggestions: he lets us believe it is OK to do what you want as long as you don't hurt anyone else; if it feels good you should do it; he tries to make you believe that fellowship with other Christians is not important. **What strategies would he use specifically against you?** Ask volunteers to share what they think their weak areas are where Satan can attack. Everyone will have different areas.

Jesus and Satan

Read the short introduction and then ask three volunteers to read the three passages and have each person write down what they say about the power Jesus has over evil.

> **Luke 4:31-37** - The demons obey and fear Jesus.

> **Hebrews 2:14-15** - Jesus releases us from Satan's power and the power of death.

> **Revelation 12:7-11** - God's people overcome Satan through the death of Jesus.

How to fight against our enemy

Look at the three pieces of advice from the Bible that help us to fight our defeated enemy. Ask the young people to work out some practical ways they can put each piece of advice into practice. **How can we help each other to do these things?** Ask the young people to volunteer some answers. Have some of your own prepared. Here are some suggestions: Be accountable to God's Word and to each other; meet regularly with God's people; help each other work on our weak areas; be prepared to point out where you see someone going astray; be willing to be corrected when someone points out a weak area. **Further Reading:** Encourage the young people this week to read Ephesians 6:10-18 and make a list of the armour God provides for us to fight our enemy. **Pray** for each other that you can resist the Devil.

Our enemy - Satan

What do you believe about Satan? Circle one of the responses.

Satan is red with a pointy tail	Yes	No	Unsure
Satan is an imaginary character	Yes	No	Unsure
God rules heaven and Satan rules hell	Yes	No	Unsure
Jesus and Satan are equal in power	Yes	No	Unsure
We should be afraid of Satan	Yes	No	Unsure

Who is he and where did he come from?

Satan (also referred to as the Devil) first appears in Eden where he tricks Eve into eating the fruit forbidden by God. Here Satan is personified as a serpent. He was probably one of God's angels who sinned and lost his position in heaven (see Jude verse 6). **Read Genesis 3:1-5.**

• **What information does this passage give us about Satan?**

Our enemy's strategies

Look at the following verses and work out what Satan does to work against God and his people:

Luke 8:12 _____

John 8:44 _____

2 Corinthians 11:13-15 _____

• **Can you give specific examples of lies or tricks Satan uses to pull us away from living the way Jesus wants us to?**

• **What strategies would he use specifically against you?** (What are your weak areas?)

Jesus and Satan

The good news for the Christian person is that Jesus has defeated Satan. God promised to overthrow Satan at the beginning of creation (Genesis 3:14-15) and he did this through Jesus. Write down what the Bible says about the power Jesus has over evil in the following verses:

Luke 4:31-37 _____

Hebrews 2:14-15 _____

Revelation 12:7-11 _____

How to fight against our enemy

Look at the advice below that the Bible gives us to fight our defeated enemy. Work out some practical ways you can put each piece of advice into practice.

Advice	What can I do to put this advice into practice?
Don't let anger lead you to sin otherwise you will give the Devil a foothold (Ephesians 4:26-27)	
Resist the devil, and he will flee from you (James 4:7)	
Be self-controlled and alert because our enemy is like a lion looking for prey (1 Peter 5:8)	

• **How can we help each other to do these things?**

Further reading: Read Ephesians 6:10-18 and make a list of the armour God provides for us to fight our enemy.

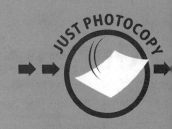

Leader's Notes
The meaning of Easter

Aim { To understand that Easter is about the death and resurrection of Jesus and to know the importance of these events.

For many people the Easter weekend has a public holiday attached to it and so many youth groups and Bible studies take a break from their usual pattern. You may like to do this study the weekend before Easter.

For your own personal preparation you may like to read all four Gospel accounts of the Easter story: Matthew 26-28; Mark 14-16; Luke 22-24; John 18-21.

Optional exercise: See page 77

What do most people associate with Easter? Have the group choose things from the list and then discuss their answers.

Note: There are some things associated with Easter that have no connection to the death and resurrection of Jesus. For example the 'Easter Bunny' has nothing to do with Easter but is a fictional character like the fictional Christmas characters of Santa or Rudolf the red nosed reindeer. The tradition of giving gifts of painted or chocolate eggs has nothing to do with Jesus. It is however thought to be symbolic of new life which comes through Jesus' death and resurrection.

What does Easter mean to you? Ask volunteers to share.

The Easter Story

Ask volunteers to share **some things they know from the Bible about the Easter story.** Share as many details as possible. Then allocate people to read aloud the ten passages from Mark's account of the Easter event. Choose volunteers for all 10 passages before reading them aloud one by one. Not everyone has to read and some people can read a couple of passages. It might help you, the leader, to write the names of the volunteers next to the passage on your sheet so you know who is reading what. There are a lot of passages but they are short. If you think this is too much for your group you could drop out some of the passages.

What do these readings teach you about Jesus and his death? Have the group discuss what the passages teach about Jesus. Encourage them to take their answers from the passages that have been read.

You may like to look through the passages and prepare some answers beforehand.

Some examples might be: It was hard for Jesus to die but he was willing (Mark 14:32-36); Jesus states clearly that he is the Christ (Mark 14:61-62) the centurion recognised that Jesus must be the Son of God (Mark 15:39).

Easter for the Christian

The death and resurrection is often referred to as the 'good news' or 'gospel'. Ask the group to rate from 1-10 the level of their certainty for each of the six statements then discuss their answers. This exercise will allow you to see how much those in your group understand what the death and resurrection of Jesus is all about. Some Bible passages that may help you in explaining this further are: Mark 10:45; Romans 3:22-25; Romans 5:12; 1 Corinthians 15:13-22.

Ask volunteers to share the areas where they are most confident and where they need help. Then challenge them to reflect this week on their response to Jesus. Suggest the further reading. You may like to all agree on one or all passages that you will each read this week.

Pray: Spend time sharing some things to pray for, then pray. Thank God for Jesus' death and resurrection and pray for those areas where people are uncertain in their faith.

The meaning of Easter

What do most people associate with Easter? Choose from the list below:

- ☐ Chocolate Easter eggs
- ☐ Family time
- ☐ Jesus' death on the cross
- ☐ Easter bunny
- ☐ Hot crossed buns
- ☐ Long weekend
- ☐ Religious holiday
- ☐ A visit to church
- ☐ Myths
- ☐ Other_____

What does Easter mean to you?

The Easter story

Easter is the celebration of the death of Jesus (Good Friday) and his resurrection (Easter Sunday).

- **What are some things you know from the Bible about the Easter story?** Think of as many details as you can.

Readings: The Easter story is found in all four gospels. Look at select passages from Mark's account that record the Easter event.

1. Mark 14:1 The plan to kill Jesus
2. Mark 14:10-11 Judas betrays Jesus
3. Mark 14:22-25 The last supper
4. Mark 14:32-36 Gethsemane
5. Mark 14:43-46 The arrest
6. Mark 14:55-56 and 14:61-64 The trial of Jesus
7. Mark 15:16-20 The soldiers mock Jesus
8. Mark 15:24-27 Jesus is crucified
9. Mark 15:33-34 and 37-39 Jesus' death
10. Mark 16:1-8 The resurrection

- **What do these readings teach you about Jesus and his death?**

Easter for the Christian

The reason Jesus died and rose again was to take our punishment for sin and bring forgiveness and eternal life to all who believe.

Look at the statements below and rate on a scale of 1-10 how you feel about each one.
(1 = I am unsure, 10 = I am really certain)

I understand why Jesus had to die on the cross	1 2 3 4 5 6 7 8 9 10
I could give a clear explanation of what a Christian believes about Easter	1 2 3 4 5 6 7 8 9 10
I know I have forgiveness for all my sin because of Jesus	1 2 3 4 5 6 7 8 9 10
I try to live my life differently from those who don't know Jesus	1 2 3 4 5 6 7 8 9 10
I have certainty that my sins are forgiven	1 2 3 4 5 6 7 8 9 10
I have the certainty of eternal life when I die	1 2 3 4 5 6 7 8 9 10

- **Which statements were you most confident about?** (Rated 6 or more)

- **Which statements do you need help with?** (Rated 5 or less)

We need to make a response to the good news that Jesus brings forgiveness through his death. This week, think about where you stand in your relationship with Jesus.

Further Reading: Today we looked at only selections from the Easter story. Try to read the Easter story this week in one (or all) of the gospel accounts: Matthew 26-28, Mark 14-16, Luke 22-24 and John 18-21.

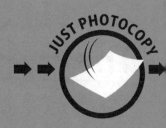

Leader's Notes
Are you too busy?

Individual Topics

Aim (This study is designed to help identify the problems with being too busy, evaluate our own level of busyness and correct the areas where we need to change.

Optional exercise: See page 77

For your own preparation also read Luke 14:16-34

Share: Ask each of the young people to share about their perfect vacation.

Life is busy

Ask the young people to discuss why they think people like to say they are busy. Prepare some of your own suggestions. Here are some to consider: people feel important if they are busy; people don't want to appear lazy; by saying you are busy you avoid having to spend time with others; by saying you are busy you avoid having to do tasks you don't want to do.

Ask the young people to circle 'agree' or 'disagree' on the list of statements and discuss each others' answers. You might like to talk about the problems with being too busy.

Too busy for Jesus

Ask for a volunteer to read **Luke 10:38-42**

What was Martha's problem? What did she need to do? The passage describes Martha as 'distracted' (from Jesus) (verse 40). She worried about too many things (verse 41). She needed to do what her sister Mary was doing and spend time with Jesus (verse 42).

Have the young people answer 'yes' or 'no' to the five statements to help them evaluate whether they are making the same mistake Martha was making. If anyone answered 'yes' to any of the statements then they are too busy. Use the following section to help them correct their busy schedule.

Dealing with busyness

Read the short introduction and then ask a volunteer to **read Mark 1:32-45**

How did Jesus deal with being busy? (verses 35, 38 and 45) He made time for important spiritual things (he made time to pray verse 35). He didn't get distracted from his task of preaching (verse 38) and stayed away from the crowds in order to not be overwhelmed by them and their needs (verse 45).

Read the suggestions for dealing with busyness. Discuss the three suggestions for correcting busyness and then ask the group to add some of their own.

It is worth noting that Martha also learned to correct her busyness. See John 11 – it is Martha who runs to meet Jesus and Mary who stays at home.

Pray for each other that we can correct the areas we need to and make Jesus our number one priority.

Are you too busy?

Share: Describe the perfect vacation. Where would you go? What would you do?

Life is busy

Often when you ask people *'How are you?'* they answer *'I am very busy'*.

• **Why do you think they say this? What do they want you to think about them?**

Circle agree or disagree to the following statements then discuss your answers:

Most people my age are very busy	Agree	Disagree
Many of my friends are stressed	Agree	Disagree
My parents are very busy	Agree	Disagree
I feel stressed most of the time	Agree	Disagree
I don't have time to do everything I want to do	Agree	Disagree
Sometimes my schedule is so full I don't get enough sleep	Agree	Disagree

Too busy for Jesus

Can you imagine being too busy for Jesus if he was to visit you? Read the following story about someone who was. **Read: Luke 10:38-42**

• **What was Martha's problem? What did she need to do?**

You might think that you would never make Martha's mistake if Jesus were to drop in to visit you. However many of us fill our lives so full with other things that we squeeze important spiritual activities out of our lives. **Are you too busy to...**

Go to church/youth group/Bible study every week	Yes	No
Spend quality time with your friends and family	Yes	No
Read your Bible and pray	Yes	No
Volunteer at your church	Yes	No
Take a day off a week from schoolwork	Yes	No

• **If you answered yes to any of the above then you are too busy!**

Dealing with busyness

Jesus was a popular guy and many people wanted his help. Read how busy Jesus was.

Read Mark 1:32-45

• **How did Jesus deal with being busy?** (verses 35, 38 and 45)

Below are some suggestions on dealing with busyness. Discuss them and then add some of your own.

1. Set a day a week when you take a break from your usual duties (i.e. study, work etc) and spend that day relaxing, spending time with others, doing Christian activities etc. A good day is Sunday for obvious reasons but it could also be a Saturday.

2. Limit your activities. You don't need to play 2 sports and learn 3 instruments. Learn to say 'no' to some things and don't fill up every day of the week with an activity.

3. When we tell people we are busy we are closing the door on spending time with them. Why not drop the word 'busy' from your vocabulary.

Some more suggestions are...

quick QUIZ

10 Commandments

Every week review the 10 commandments in order. Then ask for one fact the group learned about each commandment studied so far.

Who is Jesus: The 'I am' sayings of Jesus in John

STUDY 2 I am the light of the world

- **Why did John write the book of John?** So that we might believe Jesus is the Christ and we would believe in him and have life (John 20:30-31).
- **Who is referred to as 'I am' in the Old Testament?** God reveals himself to Moses from a burning bush as 'I am' (Exodus 3:12-15).
- **What Old Testament story is related to the passage in John about the bread of life?** Exodus 16 – God provides bread from heaven for Israel.
- **What was Jesus telling us about himself when he said 'I am the bread of life'?** He is the one who satisfies our hunger with eternal life. He is also demonstrating his divinity by equating himself with God who provided the bread from heaven in the Old Testament.

STUDY 3 I am the gate and the good shepherd

- **Why did John write the book of John?** So that we might believe Jesus is the Christ and we would believe in him and have life (John 20:30-31).
- **Who is referred to as 'I am' in the Old Testament?** God reveals himself to Moses from a burning bush as 'I am' (Exodus 3:12-15).
- **What was Jesus telling us about himself when he said 'I am the light of the world'?** The healing was a sign that Jesus is from God. He is the light by which truth and falsehood is distinguished. He shows us the way to God. It is through Jesus that we can know ('see') God.

quick QUIZ

STUDY 4 I am the resurrection and the life

- **Why did John write the book of John?** So that we might believe Jesus is the Christ and we would believe in him and have life (John 20:30-31).

- **Who is referred to as 'I am' in the Old Testament?** God reveals himself to Moses from a burning bush as 'I am' (Exodus 3:12-15).

- **What does the false teacher/false messiah come to do?** To steal, kill and destroy the faith of the Christian person. (John 10:10).

- **How is Jesus the gate and the good shepherd?** It is through Jesus' death on the cross that the way to eternal life is made possible. Jesus is the gate through which we enter eternal life. Jesus is the good shepherd who lays down his life for us.

STUDY 5 I am the way and the truth and the life

- **Why did John write the book of John?** So that we might believe Jesus is the Christ and we would believe in him and have life (John 20:30-31).

- **Who is referred to as 'I am' in the Old Testament?** God reveals himself to Moses from a burning bush as 'I am' (Exodus 3:12-15).

- **What was Jesus telling us about himself when he said 'I am the resurrection and the life'?** Jesus is the one who has power over death and is able to give life to those who believe.

STUDY 6 I am the true vine

- **Why did John write the book of John?** So that we might believe Jesus is the Christ and we would believe in him and have life (John 20:30-31).

- **Who is referred to as 'I am' in the Old Testament?** God reveals himself to Moses from a burning bush as 'I am' (Exodus 3:12-15).

- **What is the theological word used to describe God as Father, Son and Holy Spirit?** Trinity (three in one).

- **What was Jesus telling us about himself when he said 'I am the way the truth and the life'?** Jesus is the way to God, he reveals the truth about God and is the only way to eternal life. John 14:1-11 speaks very clearly about the fact that Jesus is God and that he is one with the Father.

- **Name some of the 'I am' statements by Jesus:** I am bread of life; I am the light of the world; I am the gate and the good shepherd; I am the resurrection and the life; I am the way, the truth and the life (and today's study – I am the true vine).

quick QUIZ

Practical Christian Living - James

STUDY 2 Playing favourites

- **Who wrote the book of James and to whom was it written?** James wrote to Jews who followed Jesus and were scattered from Jerusalem.
- **What is this book about?** Practical advice on how to live as a Christian.
- **What should you do when you need wisdom?** Ask God (1:5-8)

STUDY 3 Real faith

- **Who wrote the book of James and to whom was it written?** James wrote to Jews who followed Jesus and were scattered from Jerusalem.
- **What is this book all about?** Practical advice on how to live as a Christian.
- **What should you do when you need wisdom?** Ask God (1:5-8)
- **What does James teach us about showing favouritism?** We shouldn't do it (2:1); God doesn't do it (2:5) and favouritism is considered sinful along with other more obvious sins (2:9-11).

STUDY 4 Controlling the tongue

- **Who wrote the book of James and to whom was it written?** James wrote to Jews who followed Jesus and were scattered from Jerusalem.
- **What is this book all about?** Practical advice on how to live as a Christian.
- **What should you do when you need wisdom?** Ask God (1:5-8)
- **What does James teach us about showing favouritism?** We shouldn't do it (2:1); God doesn't do it (2:5) and favouritism is considered sinful along with other more obvious sins (2:9-11).
- **How does the Bible define faith?** Hebrews 11:1 faith is being sure of what we hope for and certain about what we do not see (they can say this in their own words).
- **How did Abraham and Rahab show they had faith?** Abraham was willing to sacrifice his only son and Rahab hid Israelite spies from the king of Jericho.

quick QUIZ

STUDY 5 Friendship with the world vs friendship with God

- **Who wrote the book of James and to whom was it written?** James wrote to Jews who followed Jesus and were scattered from Jerusalem.

- **What is this book all about?** Practical advice on how to live as a Christian.

- **What should you do when you need wisdom?** Ask God (1:5-8)

- **What does James teach us about showing favouritism?** We shouldn't do it (2:1); God doesn't do it (2:5) and favouritism is considered sinful along with other more obvious sins (2:9-11).

- **How does the Bible define faith?** Hebrews 11:1 faith is being sure of what we hope for and certain about what we do not see (they can say this in their own words).

- **How did Abraham and Rahab show they had faith?** Abraham was willing to sacrifice his only son and Rahab hid Israelite spies from the king of Jericho.

- **Name one of the four examples James compares the human tongue to and why?** 1. A bit for a horse's mouth; 2. A rudder of a ship; 3. A small spark; 4. A fire. (See James 3:3-6 for details)

STUDY 6 Faithfulness to God in all circumstances

- **Who wrote the book of James and to whom was it written?** James wrote to Jews who followed Jesus and were scattered from Jerusalem.

- **What is this book all about?** Practical advice on how to live as a Christian.

- **What should you do when you need wisdom?** Ask God (1:5-8)

- **What does James teach us about showing favouritism?** We shouldn't do it (2:1); God doesn't do it (2:5) and favouritism is considered sinful along with other more obvious sins (2:9-11).

- **How does the Bible define faith?** Hebrews 11:1 faith is being sure of what we hope for and certain about what we do not see (they can say this in their own words).

- **How did Abraham and Rahab show they had faith?** Abraham was willing to sacrifice his only son and Rahab hid Israelite spies from the king of Jericho.

- **Name one of the four examples James compares the human tongue to and why?** 1. A bit for a horse's mouth; 2. A rudder of a ship; 3. A small spark; 4. A fire. (See James 3:3-6 for details)

- **What does James say causes quarrels and fights among us?** Our jealousy and selfishness (4:1-2)

- **What are some instructions James gives us to resist loving the world?** See James 4:7-10 and ask the young people to think of as many of the instructions listed as they can.

10 Commandments

Optional social: Before you begin your series on the 10 commandments you could introduce the series with a social where you watch the movie 'Prince of Egypt'

STUDY 1 You must have no other gods before me

Come up with a creative way to remember each commandment in order.

This may take some time. A good way to do this is to create a picture out of every number that will help them remember the commandment that goes with it. For example the number two can be made into a picture of someone kneeling – this will help them to remember that commandment number two is don't bow down and worship idols.

NOTE: This optional exercise will replace the quick quiz. Instead of asking review questions each week like the other studies, review the 10 commandments so that by the end of the series they will know them all in order.

STUDY 2 Do not make idols

Give each person some clay or play dough (Playdoh). Have each person make a model of the thing/item they value most in their lives (this does not include people). When everyone is finished have the group try to guess what each person's model is.

STUDY 3 Misusing God's name

Break into pairs and give each pair a sheet of paper and a pencil. Each pair is to then write down as many brand names in the room as possible. (For example, the brand names for: the couch, the vacuum cleaner, the electrical appliances, the door lock etc.). If there isn't much to choose from you can widen the area to include more rooms in the building or you can limit the search to only the brand names of the clothes, shoes etc that they are wearing. Give them a time limit (i.e. 5 minutes). When the time limit is up work out:

Who found the most brand names?

Which brand name that came up the most?

Which brand name is the most well known?

STUDY 4 Remember the Sabbath

Give each person in the group a piece of cardboard the size of a regular postcard. You may like to make the cardboard look like a postcard (i.e. put a line down the middle, put 3 lines for the address and draw a box for the stamp). Ask everyone to imagine they can have a vacation anywhere they like and do any activity they like. They then must write a postcard to this group from their imaginary vacation. As well as writing the postcard they need to draw a picture on the other side. Have colored pencils for them to draw their picture and pens for them to write their message.

STUDY 5 Honor your parents

Have the group make a list of as many television shows or movies that includes a role of a parent (for example Homer Simpson). When you finish the list go through each one and discuss whether they are an example of a good parent or a bad parent and why.

optional EXERCISE

STUDY 6 Do not murder

Play a simple game you know that involves 'murder' of the people in the group. Here is an example: Murder handshake is a game where one person in the group is secretly chosen as the murderer. The group mills around randomly shaking hands with each other and the person who is the murderer will give an unusual handshake that makes it clear they are the murderer. When they shake hands with a victim, the victim will shake the hands of three more people before falling to the ground in a dramatic death. This is to avoid making it too obvious who the murderer is. The goal of the murderer is to kill everyone before they are exposed. The goal of everyone else is to guess who the murderer is before they themselves are killed. At any time in the game a person who is still 'alive' can go to the leader to guess whom the murderer is. If they guess correctly the game is over and the murderer loses. If they guess incorrectly they 'die' and are out of the game. Some rules that will make the game run smoothly are: 1. You must shake hands with people who want to shake your hand and 2. If a person who is not the murderer gives an unusual handshake and pretends to be the murderer they are out of the game.

STUDY 7 Do not commit adultery

This optional exercise can be inserted into the study. In the leader's notes I have suggested that you use this exercise just before the section on 'Jesus teaches on adultery'. Ask the young people to come up with as many movies (or TV shows) as they can where a person falls in love with someone when one or both of them are married to someone else. Then discuss the question: Based on the movies, how seriously does the world treat adultery? (What is the message the world gives about adultery?)

OR Buy up to three teen magazines. In small groups have them look at the magazines and work our what they are teaching about relationships.

STUDY 8 Do not steal

Before the study begins give everyone 5 clothes pegs that they are to peg on to the hem of their clothes (i.e. on the hem of jeans, a skirt, shorts etc.). The pegs are to be pinned to the clothing in a place where they can be easily taken. While you have afternoon tea or hang out time etc the goal of each person is to steal the pegs from the other people. They can only steal a peg if the person they are stealing from crosses some part of their body (for example if they cross their legs, their ankles, their arms, their fingers etc). You the leader will be the judge of any disputes. Only one person can steal one peg each time the person crosses some part of their body. When it is time to begin the Bible study the game is over and everyone totals their pegs to see who was the best 'thief'.

STUDY 9 Do not give false testimony

Provide 3 or 4 magazines or newspapers (or as many as you can) that profile famous people (singers, movies stars, politicians, sports people etc). Choose magazines that have the same date and cover stories about the same famous people. Have the group choose one of the celebrities that are profiled and work out some facts that contradict what is written in another magazine or newspaper. Discuss how the celebrities mentioned would feel about what was said about them.

STUDY 10 Do not covet

Buy a variety of chocolate/candy bars. Wrap them up in paper like a gift. Have the group sit in a circle (ready for Bible study) and place the gifts on the table in the centre. Have each person choose a gift and hold on to it. Choose someone to begin the game by unwrapping their gift (they are not to eat the candy bar until the game is finished and everyone has an unwrapped candy bar). The person who has unwrapped their gift may choose to keep their candy bar OR swap with the person who is next in line to open their gift. If they choose to swap, they watch the next person unwrap the gift and then swap. They cannot change their mind after the gift is opened. They will keep the gift they chose to swap. The person second in line can then choose to keep their candy bar OR swap with the next person in line. This is continued until the last candy bar is opened. This introduces the idea of desiring someone else's possession. The candy bars can be the afternoon tea.

Who is Jesus:
The 'I am' sayings of Jesus in John

STUDY 1 I am the bread of life

Have each person show the group an item that they own and have the group try to describe the owner as much as possible from that item (find out/guess what you can about them from the item). For this exercise to work best, tell the young people beforehand to bring something that they own that they would like to show the group. Alternatively, you could also ask each young person to bring one of their favourite items and have them tell the group what that item says about them.

Example: a sporting item might tell the group that the person is active, follows a certain team, likes to be a part of a team etc.

You might find yourself unprepared for this activity in which case you could ask each person to use something they are wearing or that they brought with them OR you might provide a basket of items from which people can choose.

STUDY 2 I am the light of the world

Ask everyone to close his/her eyes then hand each person an item. One by one ask them to say what they think the item is. Try to give them items that might be difficult to guess. Ask them to open their eyes and see what is in their hands. Discuss why seeing the item helps them to identify it.

In addition you could repeat/replace the exercise with holding up items behind a sheet with a light behind it so that only the silhouette is visible.

STUDY 3 I am Gate and the Good Shepherd

Hand everyone three pieces of paper. Ask everyone to write a true statement on two of the pieces of paper and on the third piece of paper write a lie. Put all the paper into a bowl. Hand the bowl around the group and one by one each person will read out one of the statements and the group will determine whether the statement is true or false. The person who wrote the statement will then give the correct answer. Continue around the circle until all statements have been read. This exercise introduces the idea of truth and deception.

OR

Make a recording of various people's voices. Play them one by one and ask the group to identify who the voice belongs to. You could play recordings of: famous people saying lines from movies or interviews, clips of songs by famous singers, people from your church.

STUDY 4 I am the resurrection and the life

If your church has a graveyard attached to it have the group walk through and find some information about the people buried there. Some information they could gather would be: Who is the oldest person buried there? Who is the youngest person buried there? Do any gravestones tell how they died? Do any gravestones have anything Christian in the inscription?

OR

Have the young people write what they would like written about them on their own gravestone OR one thing they hoped people would say about their life.

STUDY 5 I am the way and the truth and the life

Ask each person to draw a rough map outlining the way to his/her house from where the Bible study is currently meeting. If that is too difficult they could draw a map from their house to another destination (for example from their house to school, their grandparents' house, the local store etc). Ask each person to present their map to the group. This introduces the idea of finding your way somewhere.

STUDY 6 I am the true vine

Have the group go outside to the garden or walk to a nearby park. Have each person in the group choose a plant and remove a leaf, twig, flower or small branch from the plant. Go back to the room and have each person tell the group something about the plant they took their sample from. For example they might know the name of the plant, they can describe the plant (big, small, a vine, a bush etc). When everyone has finished with their description ask them what they think is going to happen to the sample that was removed. Unless the sample is somehow able to be replanted, the sample will die.

optional
EXERCISE

Practical Christian Living - James

STUDY 1 Dealing with tough times

Spend some time memorising James 1:22. For fun ways to learn the memory verse see page 78. These ideas come from the book *Creative Christian ideas for youth groups* by Ken Moser.

NOTE: Each week you may have to choose between learning the memory verse through an activity and the optional exercise as you may not have time for both.

STUDY 2 Playing favourites

Put some pictures of famous celebrities around the room. Try to have a variety of people including actors, sportsmen/women, famous people, rich people etc. Ask the young people to stand next to the pictures of the people they would want to have as a friend. Then ask for volunteers to share why they chose that person. If there is more than one person per picture you could ask the group to discuss why they chose that person and then share the answers with the rest of the group.

STUDY 3 Real faith

Set up a basic obstacle course. Arrange the group into pairs and blindfold one person in each pair. The one who can see is to lead the blind person through the obstacle course either by giving verbal instructions OR by leading them by the arm through the course. After each blindfolded person has gone through the course briefly discuss:

1. How did the person blindfolded feel?
2. In order to complete the obstacle course what did the blindfolded person have to do?

STUDY 4 Controlling the tongue

Play a game of Chinese whispers. Have the group stand or sit in a circle or a straight line. Give the first person a piece of paper with a simple sentence on it. They read the sentence and then whisper the message to the person next to them (they are not to repeat the sentence but only say it once). The sentence is passed along the line and the last person repeats the sentence. The activity can be repeated a few times. This is great way to illustrate the problem with gossip

STUDY 5 Friendship with the world vs friendship with God

Break into pairs or triplets (depending on the size of your group) and have each group make an advertisement for a product of their choice. You could also allocate some products to them. Give them five minutes to come up with an advertisement that will make having the product more appealing than being a Christian. If you had a lot of time and were really organised you could have someone video tape the advertisements and play them all.

optional EXERCISE

STUDY 6 Faithfulness to God in all circumstances

Have each person in the group show (where possible) any scars they have on their body. The scars may range from a small scratch or even a bruise to scars from operations etc. Have each person tell the story behind the scar. When everyone is finished, take a vote for which they think is the 'best' scar. This is linked to the concept of suffering which features in this study.

Individual Topics

Church

When you hear the word 'church' what do you think of? Draw your answers and then explain your drawing to the group. Take the opportunity to explain that we think of church as a building but it is really a gathering of people.

If your group meets near or on church property take the group of a tour of your church building. Try to get access to as many rooms as possible. This can help take the mysticism out of church.

Guidance

Blindfold one person in the group and give them a task to complete (for example assembling an item, finding an item in the room, completing an obstacle course). The rest of the group is to collectively shout instructions to the blindfolded person. The goal of each person shouting instructions is that the blindfolded person follows their guidance rather than anyone else's instructions. When they have completed the task (or given up completing the task because they were unable), discuss the experience.–what was helpful and what was unhelpful?

OR

Give everyone a piece of paper and a pen. Have everyone close his/her eyes. The leader gives instructions to the group to each draw a picture. The leader does not tell them what they are to draw but simply gives instructions like: move left 2 centimetres, move down 5 centimetres etc. The leader should have a simple picture in front of them that they are to draw (e.g. a picture of a bird, a picture of a chair etc). When the leader has finished the instructions have the group open their eyes and look at what they have drawn. Have them compare each other's pictures and try to guess what it is that they have drawn.

Suicide

Have each person think of one thing they hope for about the future. It can be something they hope will happen OR what they would like to do for a career. Have each person act out their future hope and have the group try to guess what it is. It is preferable that everyone acts out their answer, however, don't force them.

83

optional EXERCISE

Coping with family

In pairs or as a whole group, plan a family day that all the families in your church would enjoy. You would need to plan a day that would involve grandparents, parents, young people, little children and people in your church with disabilities. If you come up with a great idea, present it to the minister of your church as a potential church social.

OR

In pairs plan a family activity that you think every member of your families would enjoy OR plan a family activity for a family of six (two parents and 4 children of different ages)

Drugs

There are many documentaries and programs made for teenagers about the use of drugs. It may be worth a bit of time investigating a few in order to see if there is one suitable to watch with your group. This could be done at a time other than Bible study or you could choose a 10 minute segment to show before, during or after your study time.

OR

Take a vote by raising hands in the air...
Which of the following would you consider a drug?

- Coffee
- Marijuana
- Beer
- Chocolate
- Cigarettes
- Cola
- Heroin
- Potato chips
- Champagne
- Tea
- Cake

(You can add your own to the list)

Satan

Put together a 'police identikit' of an enemy. There are three ways you can do this:

1. Just like the police, have a whole pile of pictures that you could put together to make a picture of someone you could describe as an enemy. This doesn't have to be limited to the face but you can have pictures of all sorts of things. Have them arrange them to make an identikit of what an enemy is like and then have them explain it.

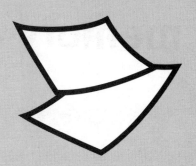
OR

2. Give each person a piece of paper and have them draw an 'enemy'. They can draw them in any way they like.

OR

3. Using a large chalkboard, whiteboard or sheet of paper have the whole group work together to draw what they think an 'enemy' is like.

Easter

Hide decorated eggs or chocolate eggs in a small area (for example the church yard) before the young people arrive for Bible study. Tell them to go find the eggs and then bring the collection back to the Bible study room. See who had found the most then eat them for your Bible study snack. The egg has been used as a symbol of new life. Explain to the young people that today's study is about the good news of Jesus death that brings new life to all who believe in him.

Are you too busy?

Prepare a sheet with a list of exercises on them. Divide the group into pairs OR divide the whole group into two separate groups. Each pair/group is to complete as many of the exercises on the list as possible. If you meet on church property or a place with some space available you can make this a scavenger hunt and have them collect items or information. Set a time limit that will mean that it is not possible to complete all of the exercises. You may like to give each item on the list a value (e.g. 10 points, 50 points etc). The exercise is to introduce the idea of having many options/things to do and the need to prioritise what is really important.

Make the list as long as possible (i.e. 25 questions/exercises) and set a time limit like 7 minutes. Some examples of exercises for the list are:

- Find out the middle names of everyone in the group and write them down (10 points)

- Write down everyone's birthdates, work out whose birthday is coming up next and sing happy birthday to them (15 points)

- Build a human pyramid with your group (20 points)

- Run around the perimeter outside the building you are in (25 Points)

- Collect 5 different leaves from 5 different plants in the garden (8 points)

memory verse
IDEAS

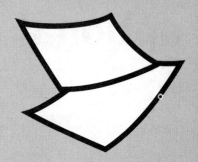

Memory Verse ideas

Memory verses are helpful to the Christian person but are also a lot of fun. Below are some examples of how to teach memory verses in a fun way. These samples are taken from *Creative Christian Ideas* by Ken Moser.

Pass the parcel

Played like the game 'Pass the Parcel'. Wrap a prize (usually a small bar of chocolate) in a piece of paper with part of a memory verse on it and so on. The group sits in a circle, music is played and when the music stops, the person holding the package removes a layer to receive a word or a part of the memory verse. Make sure the verse is in random order. When the last piece is uncovered, the whole group puts together the verse, including the verse reference.

Jigsaw puzzle

Write down the memory verse on a large sheet of paper. Cut up the paper into a number of smaller pieces and tape them under the chairs in your meeting place before the young people enter. When the time is right, tell the young people to look under their seats, then stand and form a line in the correct order of the verse. Depending on the number of people in your group, you can either divide the verse into separate words or phrases or even divide the words into syllables. Once the group is in line you can have them say the verse in order.

Verse in a circle

Have your group sit in a circle on chairs. Give each person one or two words (or phrases) of the memory verse so that the whole verse, including the reference (chapter and verse) is given to all the people sitting in the circle. Ask each person to recite their word (or words) in order, so that the whole memory verse is recited. Your goal is to say it as quickly and smoothly as possible. Say the verse a couple of times, seeing how fast they can complete the verse. It is a fun addition to have someone with a stopwatch time the group. Set a time (say 10 seconds) and see if the group can do it faster than the set time.

Here comes the twist: you then tell everyone to move a number of seats in the same direction (for instance, move three seats to their left). However, their word/s stays with the seat, so they have to find out the new word/s from the person who was sitting in that seat before.

Ask everyone to say the new word or words in order. Do this a couple of times. Have the group change seats a few more times until people are really learning the verse. A fun twist is to have everyone close their eyes when they say it. Or you could add a 'Mexican Wave'. When each person says their word, they must either stand or raise their hands.

After a couple of times of doing this, see if someone can stand up and say the verse alone.

Throw and say

Sit in a circle and give one person an item to throw (such as a tennis ball). The person with the ball says the first word of the memory verse and then randomly throws the ball to someone else. The person receiving the ball says the next word of the memory verse and throws it to someone else and so on until the verse is completed with verse reference. You can either play this until the verse is repeated successfully three times with no errors or, after a practice run, you can begin to eliminate people until you have one person left who must then recite the whole verse.

Note: With some groups, you must make a rule to throw the ball to the person and not at the person. Failure to comply means elimination from the game.

As with verse in a circle, you can have a person with a stopwatch time the group to see how fast they can go.

Word for word relay

Break your group into two (or more) teams. Give each team something to write with (a whiteboard marker, pens or chalk) and as a race against the other team, each person has to run to the board and write one word of the memory verse at a time in order. Once they have written their word, they run back to their team and give the pen to another person who writes the next word on the board and so on. The winner is the first team to finish word perfect with the reference.

It's a lot of fun as people try to remember what word comes next and they work as a team to remember each word.

Variation: for groups of 4 or less:

Give each person a different colored marker pen. Review the verse so that people can remember it. Ask each person in turn a Bible question. If they get the right answer they write up a word of the memory verse starting from the beginning of the verse. The winner is the person with the most words in their color of pen.

Blindfolds

Check to see if anyone remembers the verse, and if someone does, ask him or her to stand up and recite it. Allocate a word of the memory verse to everyone in the group, including the verse reference. You may have to give some people two or three words together if the verse is long or if there are not enough people. Hand a blindfold to each person. They then line up in mixed-up order – not in the correct order of the verse. They put on their blindfolds and must rearrange themselves so that the verse is in order. Once finished, they take off the blindfolds and recite the words – hopefully in the right order.

Notes

Notes

Notes

Notes

Other recommended resources for your youth ministry:

Studies 2 Go
By Julie Moser

Changing the World through effective Youth Ministry
By Ken Moser

Creative Christian Ideas
By Ken Moser

All available from: www.thegoodbook.co.uk